No More Tears

A Physician-Turned-Patient
Inspires Recovery

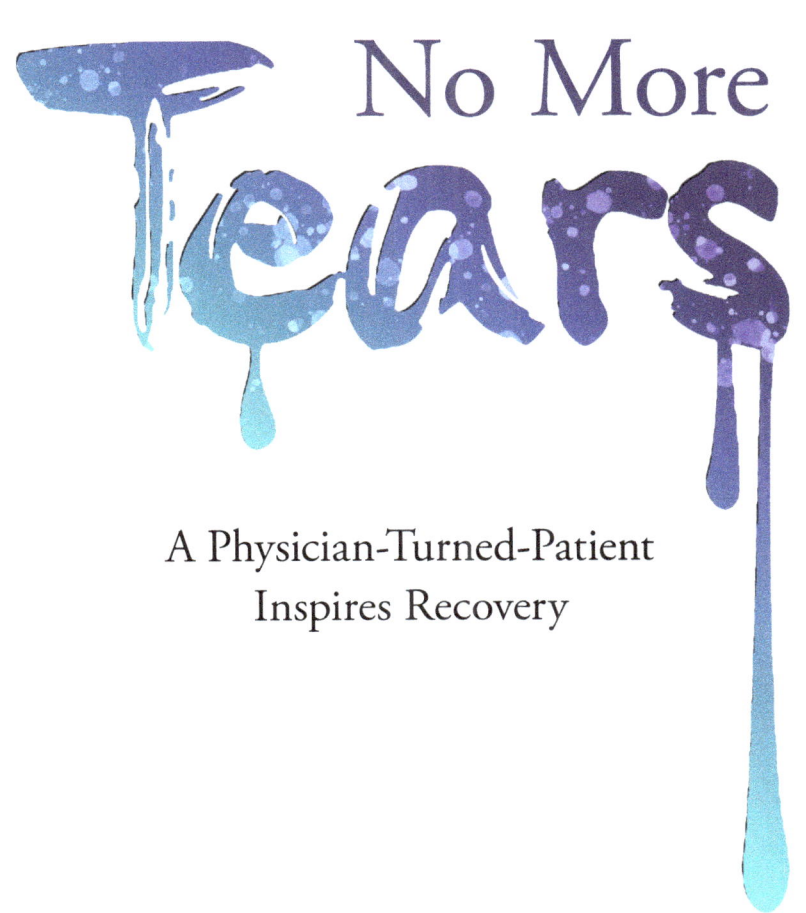

No More Tears

A Physician-Turned-Patient
Inspires Recovery

Dr. Margaret Aranda

Revised Edition 2023

Medical and Legal disclaimer: Nothing contained herein is meant to be specific medical or legal advice for any one person. Always seek medical and legal advice from your trusted health care professional or attorney, respectively.

Printed in the United States of America
ISBN 979-8-89114-007-3 (sc)
ISBN 979-8-89114-008-0 (e)

Religion / Health / Memoirs

Library of Congress Control Number: 2023915779

2023.07.22

MainSpring Books
5901 W. Century Blvd
Suite 750
Los Angeles, CA, US, 90045

www.mainspringbooks.com

Cover Art by Dr. Margaret Aranda

Dr. Margaret Aranda and her art work book cover. The book cover represents the sunrise peering through the darkness of a mountain that has been conquered. The sky is dotted with angelic skies accentuated by the blessings of heaven and the promises of an eternal life spent with God.

Dedication

This Book is Dedicated to God My Healer, My Beacon, and to His Son Who Died for Me so that I could live. And to the hope I found in others:

Dr. David Cannom and the staff at Good Samaritan Hospital, especially the Emergency Room and the Cardiology Ward staff. Thank you for keeping me alive so that I may live my life more abundantly.

Those who are disabled, especially from post-vaccine injury, Long COVID, or a traumatic brain injury: Never give up! Never!

Every spouse who stays with a disabled partner: you make love real.

Dr. Forest Tennant, DrPH, Miriam, and my pain patients: Thank you for giving me life and showing me how to be a healer.

To all my patients for COVID Prevention and Early Treatment: I thank God for making us both survivors of the impossible.

To Madi, who makes love and life real, and brings me immeasurable joy. You are My Best Girl and my reason for life.

To Carlos, who saw me through the worst times and still loves me. You are My Sunshine!

To Ed, who sharpened my sword and brought me out into the sun. God brought you to me, and you absolutely complete my world.

To Julie, my editor, thank you for completing the hardest parts of writing a book, and for doing it after your car accident. I thank God for you, and your dedication made me work harder.

To Kristie Walters, who did final edits. Your enthusiasm sparked my creativity and charged my energy to completion.

To MainSpring Books, thank you for restoring my faith in humanity by bringing this book forward as a living testimony to God's miracles.

My most special thanks to Madysson and Tanya, who gave me very special treatment in bringing these words to you. You inspire me to keep on writing!

Table of Contents

Foreword

The disease that we call dysautonomia—seemingly unrecognized fifteen years ago—is still poorly understood in the medical profession.

The causes are uncertain, the overlap with other disease entities is extensive, there is no "gold standard" diagnostic test, and the available medical and surgical therapies lack any guideline certainty. Yet without fail, the affected patients have major and incapacitating symptoms including syncope, racing pulse, postural hypotension, fatigue, nausea, and vomiting. Many end up bedridden, and depression among them seems ubiquitous. Both the patient and the physician are overwhelmed. Many opinions are sought, and more questions are asked than answered. The disease often has a long clinical course with no change and a continued search for a quick cure.

When I first met this patient, Margaret Aranda, MD, it was December 2006. She was lying in a fetal position, vomiting into the office trash can. I wish I had a videotape of what she was like then. She was thinly gaunt with black circles under her eyes. She appeared to be very fragile and ill as if there was something desperately wrong with her health. So, we performed the tilt test on patient Aranda. She promptly lost consciousness, blacking out when the table changed from the supine to the upright position. I was able to make the diagnosis of dysautonomia, dysfunction of the autonomic nervous system. I felt an impending sense of doom as if this patient was literally hanging on to life by a string.

Two years later, Dr. Aranda openly gives thanks to God for surviving one day at a time. She's survived about twenty hospitalizations, recovered from seemingly insurmountable complications of living with a peripherally inserted central catheter, and kept on fighting to live every day. She has convalesced from being in bed, throwing up every day. She has advanced from a wheelchair to a walker, from a walker to a cane, and from a cane to doing jumping jacks in my office! She exudes a vibrant aura of inspiration and has transferred it to paper for all to see.

Every path is different. Margaret found that spirituality was important in her recovery. And although most days are better thanks to the medicines and fluids, there are bad days also. She has kept the healing process alive and waits like all of us for a better understanding of this incapacitating disease.

—David S. Cannom, MD, FACC, FHRS

Acknowledgements

For life itself and this book, I thank God. So many people made me what I am today and believed in me. There is no such thing as coincidence. God continues to lead my life and direct my path. Best of all, he is equally available to be a part of your life, through his Son, Jesus Christ.

Dad, thank you for singing "That Little Old Ant," and Mom, thank you for being in my life. I am so grateful for everything.

To the University of Southern California School of Medicine Anesthesiology Department and Dr. Mohammed Nabil Rashad, Dr. Thangathuri, and to the Stanford School of Medicine Anesthesiology Department and Drs. Myer Rosenthal, Ron Pearl, Ray Gaeta, Tom Feeley, and Fred Mihm, thank you. My Residency and Critical Care Fellowship years were the best professional times of my life.

On April 10, 2022, I stood on stage at the Defeat the Mandates Los Angeles rally. Thank you to the Children's Health Defense Fund, Robert F. Kennedy, Jr., Defeat the Mandates, the FLCCC doctors, Vladimir Zelenko, MD, and all the those who protect and advocate for patients. You make me brave. Thank you, Lynne T., for being a 'reverse physician advocate' by assisting my efforts and making sure all our needs were met.

On May 5, 2022, I gave a presentation on brain fog, insomnia, and confusion at the *Optimal Health Beyond COVID Summit*. Thank you, Host Sherri Belmar, for your incredible interview and efforts. I loved working with you.

To those who do not know God, may you see Him in these pages. If you do not know Him but would like to learn more, write or visit us at https://arandamdenterprises.com. Or visit a nearby church, or listen to our podcast at https://drmargaretaranda.substack.com

Know that both Sherri Belmar and I should have died. We never should have lived long enough for you to read this book nor glean any pearls from its pages.

But it was meant to be because God saved us!

And just like he was there for us, he is there for you.

My prayer is that you find God.

God is there for you. He is waiting for you. Talk to him, reach for him and read his Word in the Holy Bible.

To accept God's Son Our Lord Jesus Christ into your heart, just pray,

"Dear God, I don't know how to know you, but you sent your only Son to save my soul and spend eternity with you. Please give me the faith to live for you as NOW, this moment, I blindly accept all that Jesus Christ did for me by dying on the cross for my sins.

I accept Christ as my personal Savior. I repent of all my sins, known and unknown. Take me into your kingdom, Lord God. Thank you for letting me be in your presence forever. I will never be separated from you.

I pray all this in the Mighty Name of Jesus Amen."

Now go tell someone!

Godfulness

I used more than mindfulness to stop my negative thoughts and turn them into positivity. I knew God was the God of Miracles and if he could neutralize a negative atom, he could turn it into a positive atom. He could do the impossible. It wasn't only that he *could* do it. It was that he *would* do it; and he would do it *for me.* I relied on my relationship with him, and the fact that he loved me.

GODFULNESS:
I knew God could take the
negative and turn it into
the positive.
But it wasn't just
that he *could* do it.
It was that he *would* do it.
For me.

No More Tears
Dr. Margaret Aranda

Others use mindfulness to be fully aware, completely present in the "now," and not overly reactive or overwhelmed by circumstances. Too overcome to be fully aware, my awareness was saturated with inabilities, difficulties, challenges, and negativity.

Others, like psychologist Scott Bishop, describe mindfulness as a "nonelaborative, nonjudgmental, present-centered awareness in which each thought, feeling, and sensation that arises . . . is acknowledged and accepted as it is."

Oh no. There was *no way* that I would or could accept anything the way that it was! Furthermore, I had absolutely *no degree of acceptance* for where I was, how I was, or what I was able or unable to do. I knew God had plans for me.

But those negative thoughts crept in, the doctors told me it was "all in my head," and my mind was filled with dread and defeat.

Realization. I first had to realize that my mind was going in the wrong direction, and it was taking my health and future with it. I could feel my mind going to negative places and my first step was to recognize that this was happening.

This small degree of self-awareness was the beginning of getting better. Not because it helped me to "reach acceptance," but it spurred me to turn the other way and get out of the rut. It compelled me to stop thinking that way, elaborating on my inabilities.

I wasn't sure how to attain the right destination, that of God's recovery and healing, but I knew it was *not* in the direction I was going.

These realizations stepped in:

I am going in the wrong direction.
This direction is wrong, and I need to make it right.
I have control over where I am going.
I am going to fix this.
I am going to change what I am doing and when I change what I am doing, I will automatically change my destination.
I am going to make a decision.
I am changing my direction now.
I will fight to get to a different place.

My first step was realizing I was going the wrong way. Exactly like being in a car and getting lost or swept away in a storm, I had to stop and think, evaluate my situation, and then make new plans.

The first thing I had to realize was that I was lost and I needed to be found. It was not just 'any kind' of lost, though. I was in the show with no one around for miles, and if I didn't get out of it soon, I could die.

Stop. It was exactly like putting a car in reverse. To put a car in reverse, the first thing you must do is realize that you must put it in reverse, because you are going in the wrong direction. That being done, I had to actively *do* something different.

To stop and go in a different direction, requires that you first *put your foot on the brakes*. You must do it. No one else can do it for you.

You just lift your foot and press on the pedal. It isn't hard. You have the power in you, because God gave you the instincts to survive, to fight for your life. You must change direction, or you may die.

By stopping, you make several statements:

I am taking charge of my situation and my life.
My future is not in the direction I was going, but in a new direction.
I am going to point myself in a new direction.
God be with me all the way! Because with him, I can do all things!

Fight. There was no other way for me to access my miracle, no other manner to dispel my conditions, but to fight them. If you are lost and need to change the direction of your car, you usually sit straight up and give yourself a burst of adrenalin. Your awareness increases, and your senses become more in tune with the environment. The adrenal glands give a pulse of adrenalin.

This "fight or flight" reflex causes our blood pressure and heart rate to go up, our pupils to dilate, and perhaps our hands or foreheads to sweat. We are attentive.

Back to getting our car to go in another direction, we cannot take "flight" by running. Instead, we "fight" by making decision after decision on where and how fast the car is going to go. That is our fight.

God gave us an entire list of fighting weapons and tools for life's challenges. In the chapters on healing and faith, we learn specific Bible verses to speak, to contemplate, and to institute. They speak of his promises, his powers, and his love for us, as well as provide instruction on how to behave toward one another. God did not give us a spirit of fear, but of power and love and of a sound mind.

My spirit began to soar. His words created and crafted a fighting spirit in me. I grabbed on to it and learned how to get "my car" pointed in the right direction.

Take Charge. Can you feel the energy? I took that negative energy and used it against itself by turning it into positive energy, a "take charge" attitude. I made the decision to take the situation into my own hands, and with God's help and a leap of faith, I would end up in a better place, in a place that he prepared for me.

"No, I am not going to think that way. I am going to pull myself out of that rut because it will get me nowhere."

Pull Back. Once I gained control of my thoughts, I learned to pull them back and then go in a direction toward positivity. I switched mental gears, backed up, and then moved forward in a new direction.

I had to control my thoughts and completely change gears.

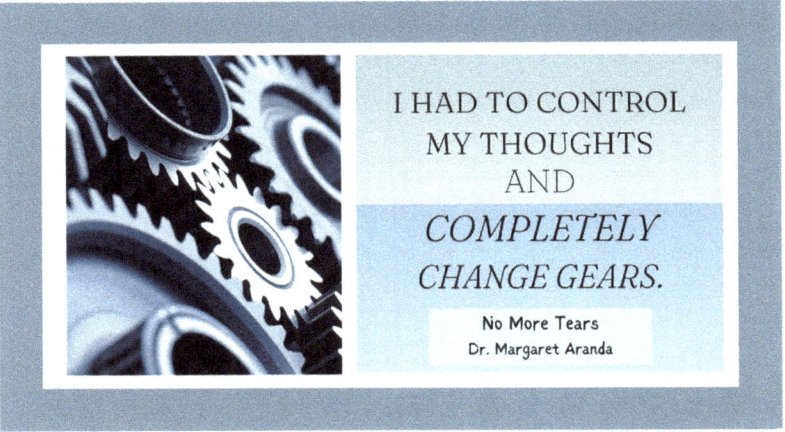

I HAD TO CONTROL
MY THOUGHTS
AND
*COMPLETELY
CHANGE GEARS.*

No More Tears
Dr. Margaret Aranda

Be Resilient. It was not an easy road. It was uphill, and there were traps and troubles ahead.

Something else would happen, like an obstacle in the road, and I would figure out a way to drive around it. I had to be resilient, learn how to "go with the flow," and be flexible and ever-changing and adapting to my new environment. It was a new flow.

Compartmentalize. No sooner than I was going in the right direction, determined to succeed, a small voice would tell me that I was never going to get off the IV, that I would have to carry it around with me for the rest of my life. I would die with a tube in my arm.

The self-sacrificial story would just get more and more negative and pretty soon my face donned despair, and my skin breathed defeat.

It could create a progressive range of negativity: from doom and self-pity to failure, defeat, and death. It was a downward spiral, and I could feel myself dying as if someone was flushing me down the toilet. I was spinning downward on a trajectory that had its own force. I had to get out. How do you start getting out of that downward spiral?

I started by placing a mental image of a wall around me and then created a zone or a compartment of negativity. I put everything in it: the negative feelings, the sometimes whispering and sometimes screaming voices that doomed me to failure. When it became unbearable unto death and I felt squashed like a bug, I told myself, *"Get out of here!"*

Sometimes I literally closed my eyes and used all my might to get out of those walls, that bad compartment.

After all, I am the architect of my own mind, the puppeteer of my own strings.

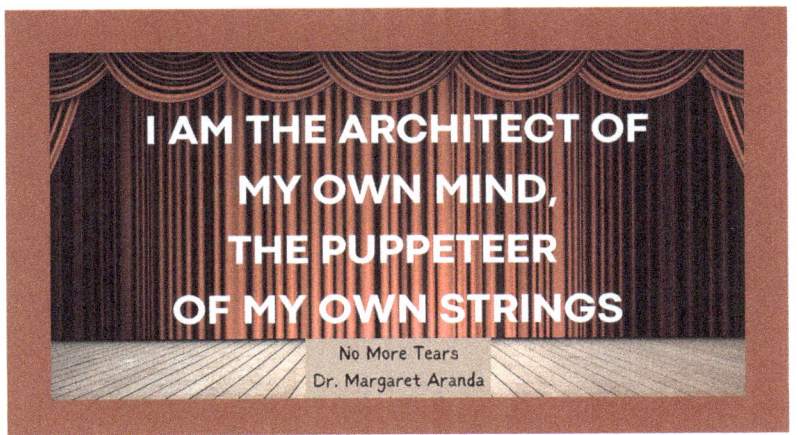

Persevere. No one can tell me who to be, what to say, or how to act. My perseverance was my possession, my gift that transcended all time and place.

If I had perseverance, that meant I would fall but I would also get up. Repeatedly, if need be, I would continue to persevere. I would get up over and over again. And I set my mind to it.

When you persevere, see yourself as "going in the right direction."

Each time another challenge blocked the road, I would sit and think very hard about ways to overcome it. If I could persevere longer than the problem existed, I would gain my desired outcome. If I sought a goal of healing and accepted nothing less, I would keep fighting for it until I found it, and then I would never stop keeping what I found.

I held on to my perseverance. It was all that I had.

I wasn't going to give up. If I had a one-in-a-million chance of surviving, *I was going to be that One. In. A. Million.*

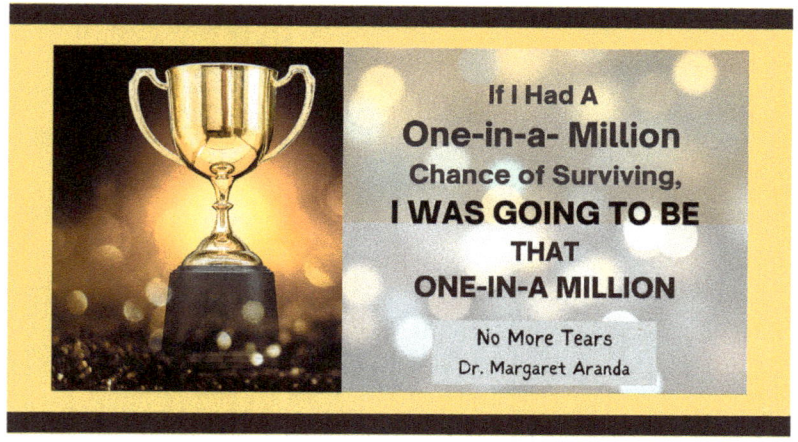

Before the Accident

From the outside, I had a joyous marriage. We lived in a 5,000 square foot house literally two houses down from the Kardashian's in a private neighborhood lined with horse trails.

Everyone liked coming to our house parties. There were free spirits, and I was an avid cook and baker. Our Christmas parties boasted a full array of food along long countertops, and they were topped off by a dinner table full of homemade desserts.

For our daughter's two-year-old birthday, I did a ladybug theme. For those that didn't wear the right colors, a door prize greeted them: a headband with boingy bug antennae. I baked her upside-down bowl cakes flipped over into ladybug decorations, and everyone had to wear black and red. I wrote my first book for her, "*Little Missy Two-Shoes Likes a Ladybug.*" I hand-sketched pastels of the times we gardened at dusk. Toddlers huddled, anticipating each page, as I did a book reading.

There was a petting zoo and one of my sisters sat in a chair while store-bought ladybugs were poured out on her lap. Initially, the toddlers huddled in a combination of curiosity and fear. Heartened by my sister's smiles that quickly transformed to glee, it was wonderful to see all the parents go inside and mingle while this live ladybug show grew to encompass little ladybugs crawling on toddler arms!

As guests departed, they each received one *Little Missy Two-Shoes* book that I ordered from a local office store. One person remarked, "A book, too?! Boy, you sure do have a lot of extra time!"

I didn't know that those days would never last. I didn't know that for over a decade, it would be the last birthday party I could create for my daughter. I didn't know that day harbored hints of failure that turned into boulders of agony.

But it is comforting to know that the memories of that ladybug party still live in us. Later, because she screamed so much on school days, we wrote Little Missy Two Shoes Likes to Go to School.

And I'm glad I went "all out." I was used to working hard, to getting up early, and searching for what the day had in store.

~ ~ ~ ~ ~ ~ ~ ~ ~ ~

Age 2: Getting Past the Edge of the Bed

"Oh boy!"

I woke up and had a quick thought. "Oh! It's time for yellow hats and green glasses!"

I was just a little two-year old toddler. I hurriedly threw the blankets back, as this bright sun-drenched room dawned on me. Each orange night-light was still on, for some reason, and the red checkered colored sheets spoke of things and happiness.

I wore dark green pajamas, those kind with a zipper and feet, with a padded sticky pad on the bottom with that kind of stuff. Rolling over on my stomach, I got positioned so that I was perpendicular to the bed, then meticulously laid my head on the middle of the bed, scooting my legs down so they flipped over the edge of the bed. This was the challenge of the day: to get past the edge of the bed, to get to greater things that were unseen.

I laid on my belly first, then grabbed onto the bedsheets with my little hands tightly clenched. My feet dangled over the edge, now my knees were over it. One hand grip loosened and moved closer tothe edge, too. Each hip pushed on the edge of the bed. Now both fists were white at the knuckles.

Slowly, ever so slowly, I let gravity pull me all down. The edge of the bed was now at my belly. My feet swung from the bed, and they inched down.

"Uh! Uh!" I grunted as my eyes looked back at the floor. I looked backwards so hard that my eyes hurt. It was morning again and I just had to do it!

"Uh!" I could not wait! I had to get out of this bed!

"Bam!" My feet hit the floor, and I went tumbling overboard.

"Uh!" My body pitched upward as I picked myself up. I was glad to be off the bed, at least. This was progress!

Quickly, I picked myself up and started running. But again, I fell.

I had been in forward motion, so my body then lost control and pitched forward, going "Boom!"

"Uh!" I was sprawled out with my hands before me, elbows down. I struggled a bit. "Uh!" I wiggled this way and that, grunting as I lifted myself again. At last, I was on my padded feet again.

"Mama! Where?" My eyes searched left and right, right and left as I made her way out of the sun-soaked room. I stumbled into the hallway, scrunching my eyes to adjust to the now dark hallway.

I peeked under the bookcase. "Where are they?" I peered under the chair. I searched. I pouted. Nothing was there. Then I had a thought. "Outside!"

I toddled over to the back door, hands smearing another set of handprints on the glass window.

"Oh boy!" I smiled. Relief. Bliss. Now I could play.

My eyes widened as I saw them together. The brother and sister cats were licking themselves in the sun, bellies up, no care in the world.

They thought they were little people stuck inside of a cat's body. I was going to make them look like really smart people. The gray one with white was Fluffy, and the pure gray one was Mattie. Today, I would dress them up in yellow with glasses, then put them in their best blue bucket, then climb up the ladder, and put them on the slide. They would slide down the slide, making funny faces and sticking their tongues out, giggling all the way down.

I would do this over and over again, just like yesterday. There was nothing else that I wanted to do. That's all I wanted, and that's what the whole day was all about.

Together, we would laugh and play the day away.

~ ~ ~ ~ ~ ~ ~ ~ ~ ~

Together,
They Would
Laugh and Play
the Day Away

No More Tears
Dr. Margaret Aranda

As a medical student, Internal Medicine intern, and Anesthesiology resident at USC School of Medicine, I worked over 100 hours a week. I was on call every third night, worked holidays and weekends, and volunteered as Vice President of the Los Angeles County—USC Medical Center House Officer's Association (HOA) representing all 1200 interns, residents, and fellows in training. One of my biggest accomplishments was getting a "bat phone" installed in the ER so they could do STAT head CT scans without waiting in line. Before that, trauma patients were dying in the hallway. I also protected the house staff housing, free meals, and a swimming pool, all of which were administratively lost after I left office.

All the way through medical training, I was also a single parent of one hell of a loving son, and together we made it through each day. He had to grow up a bit fast and learn to cook and do laundry, later joining the Navy after 911.

I graduated USC medical school and it seemed that on one day I rejoiced by throwing up my hat in the air. The next day, I drew the short straw and ended up as an intern in the big county hospital's Jail Ward.

I don't like being locked up or locked in. Neither does anyone else, let alone a four-year-old.

~ ~ ~ ~ ~ ~ ~ ~ ~ ~

Age 4: Don't Panic

It was after just a few minutes that I heard it.

"Wa-a-a-a-ahhh!" "Mo-m-m-y!"

I ran to the bathroom door, white and tall. And locked. I checked it again. It was really locked.

He was just four years old, wailing like he was dying, one fingernail at a time.

"Don't panic!" I said, with my mouth by the doorknob, squishing my lips in the tiny airspace therein.

"Use your head!"

"Wa-a-a-a-ahhh Mommy!" Louder now, as if I never said one word. How was he ever going to hear me if he was screaming so loud? This was my conundrum. It was double sided: I wanted him quiet for myself and for him, and I was also desperate to quiet him down, lest the neighbors think that I was torturing the poor child. Despite all, the screams continued.

Actually, they were 'wails.' Worse than screams.

"Wa-a-a-a-ahhh!" "Wa-a-a-a-ahhh!"

. . . and then louder, "WA-A-A-A-AHHH!"

I called this Level Two crying. A deeper, more morose effort was clearly heard. Then the «Mo-m-m-y» turned into «MAMA!! MAMA! I need you! Mmmm-aaaa-Mmmmm-aaaa!»

Oh my.

For a full five minutes, they continued. I had sweat under my arms, and I just wanted him to take a breath so I could get two words in.

"Don't panic! Use your head!"

Finally, finally, finally, when we were both so spent that it hurt, he talked to me.

"Huh?"

I calmed him down. I told him to put his fingers over the lock thingie that stuck out.

"Huh?"

I explained that it had to turn 'sideways' instead of 'up and down.' I felt so stupid explaining this to a 4-year-old. How was he going to understand?

I calmly talked him through it and suddenly, 'Pop!' The door opened.

He flew into my arms, sweaty, red face, panicked face, covered in a cloud of effort like Pig Pen from Peanuts.

It was as if nothing in the world could be any better at that very moment. Because nothing in this world could have been any better at that very moment.

~ ~ ~ ~ ~ ~ ~ ~ ~ ~

Freedom can be breathtaking, and we learned that each day going into Jail Ward was going to be met with a very warm welcome at leaving it.

Sometimes the inmates would come in from County Jail (CJ) in orange prison suits, chained to one another by the ankles. They shuffled into the elevator, shuffled out, and walked by a lineup of Sheriffs that did an awesome and outstanding job of protecting us. In the beginning, I thought both they and the LAPD were harsh to inmates, sometimes landing them on the floor restraining their arm up their back. I almost spoke up the first time, but quickly realized this was a different culture, a different world.

On the first day's orientation, the director told us that if any of the inmates took one of us hostage, we would be in "lock down." We looked at one another and gulped. We resigned to just literally survive the month and walk out of there alive.

~ ~ ~ ~ ~ ~ ~ ~ ~ ~

Age 6: Glistening in the Moonlight

Sheriff John was a Sheriff. He wore a shiny badge, shiny boots, and a brown cowboy hat with a Sherriff's golden buckle that covered up all his hair. I never saw his hair.

Every week on television in Los Angeles, California, he would sing, "Put another candle on my birthday cake," as a yummy carousel cake spun around, and the camera went in for a close up. There were lions and tigers and bears on the carousel. Roar! They spun around and around, as if dancing in their own world, oblivious to the rest of us. They were only focused on going up and down, down and up, chasing one another around and around. They were majestic each in their own way. Royal.

I was six. I closed my eyes really, really tight and I thought that if I closed them hard enough and "thought" extra hard, I could turn into one of those gorgeous animals. And so, I did it.

I closed my eyes and I blinked just like that Genie on TV that has a cute little home in a bottle with red draperies, black bedsheets and golden tassels all about. I closed my brown eyes and I thought so hard that I expected to open my eyes and literally be in the body of a great lion.

My eyes crinkled. At first, I could feel nothing. After a time, I could definitely feel my tail growing, and I thought, "It must be almost time to open my eyes." I scrunched my eyes more now, as I wanted to make sure that nothing would be missing. I wanted to be sure as ever that my teeth would be long and sharp, that my claws would glisten in the moonlight. "There has to be nothing better than glistening in the moonlight," I thought, momentarily forgetting that I was still a girl.

My mouth cracked a gentle smile as again, my tail was starting to come out. I waited for it to grow fully and sassy, still tightly crunching my eyes.

Now I thought I was ready to open my eyes, without getting it wrong. Certainly, I was on the right track. Ever so painfully slowly, I opened my eyes.

At first, they ached from squinting so hard in my fervent prayer. I saw the light of day as they opened, and there he was again! I glared closer, disbelief covering my entire body. Now Sheriff John was reading from a piece of paper!

"Wait!," I thought, "I'm not supposed to know what a piece of paper is!" My eyes began to blur as the first tears started forming. "I must not be a lion!," I shockingly reflected.

He wouldn't stop to care about my plight. "Linda, Joanne, Sarah, Tom, Edward, and Brian! Wishing you all a Happy Birthday!" said Sheriff John, happy as could be, as if nothing else was as important and completely missing my predicament.

I was disappointed, hurt, and well, I was sad. I was shocked. "How come it didn't work? I can't believe it didn't work!" I was already six years old, the smartest one in my class, and I got Gold Stars on my tests! What did I do wrong?

I sunk in the living room sofa. I cried big tears of reality and disappointment. And I learned, as we all do, that I couldn't just change into a lion whenever I wanted to. I kept it to myself until just now. I'm only telling you because I know you won't tell anyone else.

~ ~ ~ ~ ~ ~ ~ ~ ~ ~

I was petite, 5'4" and 115 pounds, with just a shadow of strength compared to the inmates. On the first day, when a large, burly inmate started yelling at me, three Sheriffs quickly showed up, stepping it up a notch and yelling right back. The Sheriffs were imposing, and to me they seemed to be seven feet tall. No one ever talked back to them.

It was then that I realized the inmates generally do not play by the same civilized rules of the outer world. If they could, they would strangle me. If I was without Sheriff's protection, they could harm me.

Gangs, gunshot wounds, and stabbings were commonplace.

~ ~ ~ ~ ~ ~ ~ ~ ~ ~

Age 30

I was Vice President of LAC-USC Medical Center's House Officer's Association (HOA) and we regularly met with the hospital Chief of Staff and the L.A. County Board of Supervisors.

In 1990, they wanted to take away the house staff housing, and pour cement into the swimming pool. They also wanted to take away free food in the Doctor's Dining Room and to save on gas, they expected us to carpool with one another to the hospital.

We met with the Board of Supervisors in a heated argument on the latter, convincing them we did not need to carpool because we saved a commute three days a week by spending the night in the hospital. They were completely out of touch and unaware we pulled call nights, having no set "hours" of work.

The medical center was the second largest medical facility in the world. It was simply huge, boasting the same hospital steps that are seen on the soap opera, General Hospital. This was the place.

Women's and Children's Hospital was separate, and we had to walk down the hill to do anesthesia for laboring women: epidurals, spinals, and general anesthesia. Incredibly, we carried our "drug box," a metal locked box of liquid fentanyl, demerol, morphine and thiopental in this box. Its street value was thousands of dollars, which gave me a fear of being assaulted.

As I walked carrying my drug box, it was obvious that I was a doctor in training. Up the hill would come four teenaged males together in a pack towards me on my walk down, and I didn't like having to pass them on the same sidewalk, even in broad daylight. When my work was done for the day, it was usually after dark, and I was too afraid to walk back up the hill. Instead, I went to the ER and asked the LAPD to drive me in a 'black and white' up to my car in the doctor's parking lot. No matter how long it took, no matter how tired I was, I never walked by myself in the dark.

My fears were justified. A medical student had been killed in the nearby park; another pregnant resident physician had been assaulted in the parking lot. The HOA asked the hospital staff for statistics on assaults; we were not granted access to any data.

Shortly thereafter, in the evening after a long day, the doctor's dining room was long closed for dinner, so I had to eat in the regular cafeteria. I sat in the nearly empty cafeteria, looking up from eating hot chicken soup, when I heard a woman's chilling scream and a man's arguing voice.

There was bright red blood on the floor, and a female nurse was laying prone, bleeding arterial gushes from the neck. Reportedly, a homeless man had asked her for a dollar. She reportedly said no.

A large group of men dragged her on the floor, head-first, to the ER. The blood dragged on the floor leaving a thick trail behind her. I was left staring.

Wasn't the HOA talking about assaults on hospital grounds, asking our Director to make us aware of the prevalence of physical assaults on house staff? Isn't this what we were trying to prevent?

Her carotid artery was punctured. She was taken to the Operating Room and she survived. Thank God it occurred there and not in the parking lot, or she may not have survived.

After graduating medical school and throwing my graduation cap into the air, the next day I was just an Intern.

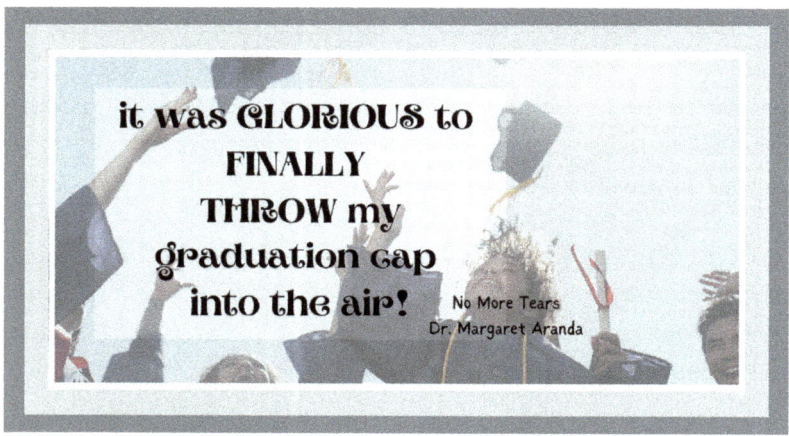

I did the 'scut' work: drawing blood, taking urine samples and doing the dipstick on them myself. I even took blood and let it go into capillary tubes, then spun it on a centrifuge to determine the hemoglobin and hematocrit levels on my patients.

I was busy. I was busier than busy.

When Thanksgiving rolled around, I was off for the day, but it was a post-call day, so I had been up for 24 hours. I slept before going to my Dad's house for dinner, and after eating, I slipped away and went straight to sleep on the first available bed. My family jokingly said all I did was sleep after gatherings, and they were right. I was post-call. I had no choice.

I was out of Jail Ward now, rotating in the ER. A new 24-hour Observation Unit was set up to handle triage, the sending out of patients to various destinations. One of my patients was an alcoholic with seizures, and he had wandered off the Unit. He wasn't in bed, and I could not find him. I looked around the circular unit desk station, and there were two nurses there. I told them I was leaving to go look for my patient.

No one would have thought that it was a wrong thing to do.

I walked down the hallway and immediately spotted him, as he was 6 foot 6 inches and wearing a hospital gown. He limped along, pushing his IV pole down the hallway. I thought maybe he was going outside to smoke a cigarette, as was not unusual for some patients. I hoped he was not going out to do drugs. Or deal them. I called him by name.

"Mr. Patterson, there you are. I need you to come back to your room with me," I said gently.

He looked down on me, because I'm only 5'4."

He said "Okay."

Together we headed back toward the Unit. I didn't think anything at all. I was on his left, and he walked behind me and slightly to my right.

Out of the corner of my right eye, I saw his arm come up behind me a bit, and I thought that he was going to rest his hand on my shoulder. Since he had a seizure, I thought well, that would be okay because maybe he is tired or something.

But no, instead he wound his elbow around my neck. He lifted my body off the floor, and I could feel that my toes were not even touching the ground.

I couldn't scream. I couldn't move.

I thought that if I tried to fight or kick, he would break my neck. There was nothing I could do. So, I dangled.

But after a bit, I was suffocating. I had no control. I could only wait to be rescued. Time ticked. I held my breath, or did I? Maybe I held it on purpose so my neck would not break. All I remember is that I couldn't move.

And I couldn't breathe.

"Hey!" I heard a man's scream.

Then there was a brief scuffle.

Eventually, I was freed to the floor.

Everyone concentrated on the patient. Since he was my patient, I called for some valium IV. He needed sedation and because of his history of seizure, this would help ensure that he would not have another seizure. He was on around-the-clock benzodiazepine medication and had missed his evening dose. After it arrived, I pushed the drug into his IV myself.

Once that was done, I felt light-headed. I wasn't feeling well.

Then the attention shifted to me.

"Your face was blue!" said Mark, the male nurse who had apparently jumped on the man's back to rescue me.

Mark said, "I'm in the Army Reserves, and he had you in a military headlock! All he had to do was to scrunch his arm just so . . . and POOF! Your spinal cord would have been severed!"

There was nothing to say except—thank you. Wherever you are, I still thank you.

~ ~ ~ ~ ~ ~ ~ ~ ~ ~

From then on, I couldn't do a lot of things other moms could do. I couldn't run and jump, go swimming, or take him to the park. I was unable to play hide and seek outside in the twilight.

~ ~ ~ ~ ~ ~ ~ ~ ~ ~

Age 7: The Pigeon Boy,
The Suction Bush, and The Darkness

They were real pigeons. They lived in a huge metal cage with a wood roof, worn and tattered but nonetheless, it was home. I tippy-toed to peer in at the eggs, the feathers, and of course, the poop. It smelled, but not too bad. There was plenty of fresh air.

The pigeons cowered a bit, restless and uneasy with someone else's eyes on them. I moved along the cage, from left to right, all the way down the line. They had food and water, I noted, and they could surely fly out the top of the cage any time they wanted. There was a hole of freedom at the top.

They all belonged to my best friend, Anne. Anne had a really nice Mom and Dad, and a big brother, too. The big brother did things like play after dark, and he liked to play with bugs, too. He said that the pigeons were his, which started Anne screaming at him, saying, "No! They are mine!"

He said that they were "homed," and he was "the one that homed them, so they belonged to him." Huh. They could fly away any time they wanted, he said, then come back. They liked to come back home again, that's why they were "homed." I thought that if he "homed" them, then maybe he was right, and Annie was wrong. It seemed like they should be his, maybe, right?

I was only seven years old, and this was going to be the first night that my Mom let me spend the night with anyone. Anne was my best friend, and had been my best friend since kindergarten, so we were best friends for three whole years, positively a lifetime! We played hopscotch together before school, our desks were next to one another in class, and we ate lunch together, too. We called ourselves "Bestest Friends." Bestest Friends Forever. In fact, it seems we invented BFFs.

The back yard was wondrous and delicious. There was a huge bush in front of a hill, and trees were scattered about so that there was plenty of room to play, run, catch ball, or do jump rope. Neighbor kids whose names I didn't know just walked on over, because there was no fence around the property. It was just wide-open space.

The sun was going down now, casting a sideways shadow on the hill. Crispy air surrounded them, but it was fine because they were running around so much that the cold was unnoticeable. It just wasn't even cold.

It was getting dark, and I was not used to playing outside after dark. It was beginning to get kind of scary, and the other kids wanted to play Hide and Seek.

Well, I wasn't about to be a big baby about it, so I said "okay." Since this was my first night away from home, I really did not want them to think I was a baby. Another wave of neighbor kids joined in, and it was turning out to be a glorious night. Anyway, if everyone else's mom let them stay out in the dark to play, then it must be okay.

No one knows how it started, really. Somehow, we were in front of a huge, dark green bush with soft leaves and flexible branches. We decided it was a 'suction bush.' Whenever someone unwittingly walked by, the bush 'sucked' them in, and their arms and legs were left to hopelessly flail in the darkness. It took someone else to help them out, because the suction was so powerful.

Relentlessly, I shrieked with laughter as a Rescuer helped me out of the dark, ominous suction bush. For hours, neighbor kids took turns first getting sucked into the bush and then scouting it to be certain no one was sucked into it.

Sometimes, the Rescuer would be Anne, and I could see Anne's big eyes peering at me and then pulling me out. We struggled together, with Anne's grip tightening around my wrist, then my forearm, then my elbow. Pulling and pulling, until finally I was free. Other times, a random hand would pop into my face and grip my nose. It was dark, so then at least I knew where it was and I could grip that hand and then that wrist would pull, pull me out. I noticed that when a boy pulled me out, especially if it was Anne's brother, who I now named the Pigeon Boy, it was different. He didn't need to climb up my arm to get a grip, no. Instead, he just effortlessly and deliberately pulled me out in one full sweep.

I started to close my eyes to see if I could tell who it was that was pulling me out of the bush, and I got it right every time I guessed it was The Pigeon Boy. He had big hands with fat fingers, this Pigeon Boy. I mean, he was strong. His fingers swallowed my wrist and pulled me to freedom in one huge Swoop! of strength. Pow! I was out in one second! That was the first time I really knew how strong a boy could be.

I jumped in the bush again. It was fun to just close my eyes and wait to see who would come for me. Again and again, The Pigeon boy gripped me strongly as I shrieked in horror at the bad Suction Bush. Again and again, I was reduced to tears and laughter when I was rescued. I was breathless! And again and again, that Suction Bush pulled me in, as if that was its sole mission.

I rubbed my eyes now, as they were tearing in the darkness, and I felt tiny crumbs of soil on my cheeks. Then I looked at my own slender hands. They had strips of dirt on them, as the bushes rubbed off on me. My brown hair was strewn and tossed about, riddled with pieces of leaves, tangles, and knots. My blue pants and matching blue and white shirt were so dirty that my first thought was that my mother would be mad if she could see me now. But the whole night was fun, and I continued to laugh. It was so fun that I forgot about my mom just about the same second that I realized how much fun I was having. The Suction Bush, The Pigeon Boy, and the Pulling and Pulling went on!

It went on for hours and hours and I just wanted the night with its impending bedtime to never come. Much later, when we could barely see in the dark, us Bestest Friends ran away from that mean old bush, laughing because we were smarter than it.

I had never stayed out so late to play, I had never gotten so completely dirty, and I had never played that close to a boy. I wasn't going to mention to anyone that it was past my bedtime, because I did not want to give anyone the idea that it was time to stop playing (or that I was still a baby, of course). I told myself to stop thinking about stopping playing. And I played as if playing would never end.

~ ~ ~ ~ ~ ~ ~ ~ ~ ~

I told myself
to stop thinking about
stopping playing.
And I played as if
playing would never end.

No More Tears
Dr. Margaret Aranda

I played,
and I played.
And I learned
how to
let the night
go on
forever.

No More Tears
Dr. Margaret Aranda

After returning to complete my internship in a neck collar, I could no longer go up and down the stairs, much less open and close their huge fireproof doors. The department accommodated me by assigning me to one-floor rotations so I could just be in one floor.

Because of that, I rotated through oncology twice, doing difficult blood draws and IVs, as well as doing a plethora of lumbar punctures. Back then, I was doing everything by myself and without supervision except for the beginning of each day, when the resident and Oncology staff rounded with us. My one-ward rotations gave me specific experience in oncology, cardiology, Jail Ward (I had to do it a second time), and I worked the first month when a new HIV Ward opened.

In the middle of my residency at USC, I applied for, was accepted, and then transferred to Stanford anesthesiology residency.

Later I would be accepted into their Critical Care Fellowship. Being a Hispanic woman in anesthesiology was easy at Stanford. What I loved the most about residency was that I wasn't the only woman in the rest room. In stark contrast to USC anesthesiology, about fifty percent of residents were women. It was good to be one of many, treated like the rest, and that is all I ever wanted.

Because I never grew up wanting to be a doctor, my prayer was for God to lead my direction and show me the way to go. He answered my prayers by giving me official acceptance into only one Medical School (ORU), one residency (USC), and one Fellowship (Stanford). Everyone thought I was crazy for doing it this way, because everyone else was flying to 20 interviews and getting multiple acceptances. I had just one job offer after Fellowship: the University of Pennsylvania.

The same as happened to me in medical school, I had to repeated core rotations at the new institution, Stanford, after already completing them at USC. I received… "double experience" Ob/Gyn, cardiac anesthesiology, preoperative clinic, pain management, pediatrics, and orthopedics. The biggest difference between USC and Stanford was twofold: I did more procedures and got less sleep at USC, and I got more academics and more sleep on call nights at Stanford. It was the best of both worlds. I was so used to getting paged all night at USC, that upon transfer to Stanford, I remember waking up asking the Operator to beep me, to check and see if my pager was working!

I loved the ICU and felt at home there. Everyone was nice to me, and it was a monumental joy to teach the medical students and residents. Each day had its own challenges and I worked hard every step of the way.

Of all the things I loved about Stanford, it was my Attendings, the nurses, and Life Flight.

No More Tears | Dr. Margaret Aranda

Of all the things I liked about Stanford, it was LifeFlight

Dr. Myer Rosenthal was an icon, as was Ronald G. Pearl, now Chair of the Department. Drs. Tom Feeley and Fred Mihm were incredible, as were the pulmonary and nursing staff. I got to do Life Flight and go by helicopter to pick up ICU patients and bring them back to Stanford ICU. This was a dangerous job, especially on a rainy day, and years later, one helicopter crashed and killed everyone on board. It was incredibly sad.

The ICU was a family, with doctors, nurses, pharmacists, respiratory therapists, and nutritionist all working together for good, many of them for decades.

My ICU Fellowship experience was phenomenal at Stanford, with post-surgical and medicine patients on ventilators, many intravenous drips, and a lot of didactic teaching. I was one of just three in the nation selected to be a Fellow, and the privilege was constantly palpable. As much teaching as I received during residency, it felt like there was more teaching in that one year of Fellowship than in the previous three! My brain was at full capacity, and I loved the way the nursing staff and Attendings treated us.

As I was growing up, I never wanted to be a doctor. I always told myself I could not stand the sight of blood and I had no interest in even being a nurse. I was used to working as the second oldest in a big family, as there were perpetual chores: laundry, cooking, dishes, homework, clothes, lunches. My very first job was at age 8, when my mom gave us a plate of cupcakes and told us to go sell them to the neighbors.

~ ~ ~ ~ ~ ~ ~ ~ ~ ~

Age 8: Selling Cupcakes

In 1968, it was okay to go door-to-door with a plate full of cupcakes. We sold them for 5c each. I don't think we needed the money, but with six girls and one boy, maybe my Mom just wanted us to do something productive.

My older sister stayed home, leaving me with Martha and Louise. That also left me in charge. Martha was one year younger than me, and in turn, Louise was one year younger than her.

We were properly dressed in white socks and shoes, sleeveless plaid shirts, and crisp pants that had a line down the middle as my Mom liked to iron. Our hair had ribbons and bows, our teeth were brushed, and we were ready to go.

We lined up in the avocado green-and-mustard kitchen, waiting for Mom to give us the cupcakes. We thought this would be fun, although it wasn't clear who would get the money. Figured it would just go to Mom, but why did we need money, anyway? We shrugged our shoulders in unison as she walked into the room.

She wasn't tall, but to us, being kids, she loomed above us. We straightened up. She gave us a huge plate of cupcakes that we had not even helped to make or decorate. She did it all. She gave us detailed information on what to say when the person opened the door, how to take money, and then she instructed us to give a napkin to each person, too.

So, I had two plates of cupcakes, Martha had the napkins, and Louise held nothing, so she opened the door. We delineated a specific plan that if the house had a screen door, Louise would be the one to open it so that people could see the cupcakes when they opened their front door. With that last detail clear, we agreed it was time to leave.

So off we went!

The outside air greeted us with anticipation and excitement as we made our way with a variety of cupcakes. It was a hilly and green neighborhood in Redondo Beach; our house boasted a gigantic magnolia tree. We had two plates, each colored with blue, pink, green, yellow, and then a coconut cupcake. There were multicolored sprinkles and little red sugar flakes that melt in your mouth right away. We didn't get to eat any before we left, so we briefly contemplated just eating one or two. But we quickly discarded that idea because there were three of us and it would be a noticeable difference if we didn't get the right amount of money before we went home.

The three of us went, the three "big ones," walking up the street, then around the corner on a wondrous crisp Saturday afternoon. As usual for the month of July, it was overcast, and droplets of water were visible in the air as we walked through them with ease. If we weren't on an official journey, we would have looked for cigarette butts on the ground and pretended to smoke, because when we exhaled, 'smoke' from the mist came out. It was fun to pretend to be a grownup.

So we went to the first door. A nice lady opened the door, peered at the cupcakes with glee, and bought a few. She was wondering what we were going to do with the money, so we just told her we were giving it to our mom. It didn't occur to us that we could be making the cupcakes ourselves and saving the money to give to the poor, or to build a treehouse or something. She took the blue one, the coconut one, and the pink one. We had 15c. Off we went to the next house.

We did this again and again. Several people were not even home, and we had to walk a long way to get from one door to the next. I guess the houses were farther apart than they looked. Or maybe the plates were getting heavy. Three more houses, 7 more cupcakes sold.

The sun was coming out now, heating up the place, and we were getting tired, and hungry. The jingle of nickels and dimes in my pocket did nothing to make us feel any better.

I put one plate under the other when one plate sold, because it was easier to carry. But that made for one heavy package that was getting heavier and heavier with each step. My arms were tired. We were really hungry now, and we thought maybe we could lie and say a few of them dropped. We were just discussing the plan, when the next door opened to our knock.

The door was already opened, and we looked up to give our speech and ~~~~~~ uhmmmm . . . ~~~ @P(*%Y(@T)#!*%^_\$(@*&!!!

Our eyes opened more than they could open! We gasped! The lady had a mustache! What!? It was a real mustache! It was thick and gray and it went up on the ends. It was a real live mustache on a lady! She was old, peppered gray hair and I don't know how tall she was or what she was wearing or what she said, and actually I don't know if she said anything at all.

For an instant we thought we were being punished by God for thinking of lying about the cupcakes. Or maybe she was a witch! Maybe she had evil powers and she would try to grab us and pull us into her house and stick us in a brew of some kind!

We glanced sideways at one another. We didn't say a word. I simply dropped the plate of cupcakes on the ground as I jetted away, and one cupcake after another was toppling down, down to smash crumble, oh my!

We ran! We ran and we ran all the way home. We weren't laughing, we weren't tired or hungry. We weren't being mean; we were just plain scared. We ran and we ran and we ran.

When we got home, we couldn't help but tell mom about the lady with the mustache. She didn't know if we were making it up, but the details were certainly too fine to be a lie. Besides, we all told the same exact story.

At eight, I learned to sell cupcakes as a job, but more memorably, I learned that a lady could have a mustache.

~ ~ ~ ~ ~ ~ ~ ~ ~ ~

On many occasions growing up, my dad had remarked to me, "I love going to work! I can't believe I get paid for it! When I leave, I can't wait to get back the next day, and when I am there, I love every minute!"

For decades, I was too little to understand what he was talking about but when I was at Stanford, I knew what he meant.

On many occasions growing up, my dad had remarked to me, "I love going to work! I can't believe I get paid for it! When I leave, I can't wait to get back the next day, and when I am there, I love every minute!"

For decades, I was too little to understand what he was talking about but when I was at Stanford, I knew what he meant.

From there, I went on to the University of Pennsylvania and was Assistant Professor in three departments: Anesthesiology and Perioperative Medicine, Surgery and Traumatology, and Radiology. I was recruited primarily to attend in the Surgical/Traumatology ICU, and there was a lot of teaching time. I did anesthesia in Day Surgery, worked Preoperative Clinic, published research regarding patients inthe Intensive Care Unit, Pain Management, and collaborated with Johannes-Gutenberg University anesthesiologists, physicists, and radiologists by doing bench research on lung injury with CT scans.

My father, a mathematician and physicist by schooling, would have been particularly proud to see me working with hyperpolarized ^{3}Helium MRI of the lungs, an oxymoron because there is too much water in the lungs to do an MRI. They were only visible after helium was hyperpolarized to a higher spin of ^{3}He, by using a wide-beam laser light we generated in the lab. Together with physicists and radiologists, we wrote $3 million in NIH grants.

During 911, our Anesthesiology Department Chief offered me a faculty position as Chief of Anesthesiology at the Philadelphia VA Medical Center. Working with Veterans was always a pleasure and I had done so since an undergraduate premedical volunteer as President of the Sepulveda VA Pre-Med Club (see Appendix photos).

When we were locked down that afternoon of 911, I offered to work ER, OR, ICU, or any floor, but of course no one survived to get flown to Philadelphia. The Chief of Staff wrote me a nice thank-you letter, and I left the University of Pennsylvania, transferring to be Chief of the Surgical Intensive Care Unit at the West Los Angeles Veteran's Administration.

My father had Alzheimer's.

~ ~ ~ ~ ~ ~ ~ ~ ~ ~

AGE 1: I Had No Fear

It was my Father. I knew it was him, and I had no fear.

My Father held me, and his arms and his scent were familiar to me. In fact, I can still smell him if I close my eyes and reminisce just a little bit. There. I can do it now. I know he is gone but it's almost like he is just next door, always there.

It was a summer day, sun beaming into my grandmother's San Antonio living room. The smell of bacon and coffee emanated throughout the room, boastful of the percolator that gurgled and puckered its congenial hellos to the morning. My uncles and aunts were in the room, as well as my cousins, and the room hummed with conversation here and giggles there. Children were running about, in and out the front door, slamming the screen door behind them. The reason why I remember who was there, is because I was looking down on them all.

I could sit straight up, and no doubt my curly dark brown hair was tossed all about. I didn't care about anything except my father. He told everyone to "Watch!" My mom echoed the usual, "Oh no, honey, you're not going to do that thing again, are you?" She was simply horrified and really, she was quite disgusted. My Dad told her to relax. She just stared at us.

I closed my eyes and tried with all of my might to hold in the excitement. I was sitting in his hand now, his right hand.

My father had me.
He was
My Father.
I knew him
And I had no fear.

No More Tears
Dr. Margaret Aranda

Slowly, ever so slowly, as I was sitting on the edge of his hand, he started to lift me up. He lifted me up! and up! and up! and up! Straight up to the ceiling we went, and I closed my eyes and I held in the burst of exclamations as tight as I could. Up! Up! I went, dreaming of everything and dreaming of nothing. I was on the edge, and that was where I was going to stay. I had no fear. My father would hold me up, just like he always did. I could do this. I knew I could.

My father had me. He was my father. I knew it was him, and I had no fear.

~ ~ ~ ~ ~ ~ ~ ~ ~ ~

My Father Had Alzheimer's

My father was a gentleman who loved his children, sending all seven of us to Catholic School. When I was in kindergarten, he took off his glasses and using them as a magnifying glass, he pulled a dried magnolia leaf off the tree. He then matter-of-factly proceeded to hold it up to the sun and burn a hole through the leaf. It started slowly with a black circle that billowed a string of smoke, then got larger and larger.

As I saw the smoke go up and the hole getting larger, that impressed me as my first biology "magic trick" science experiment. It was truly magical to me, how sunlight could burn a hole in a dry leaf. It impressed on me how the world we lived in had things in it that we could use for heat, and other needs. This was my father's brand of creativity, and he was constantly inventing things.

Because of him, I learned to reinvent myself. More than that, he taught me how to believe in myself. He also used to say to me as a little girl of about nine years of age, "Don't you ever let anyone say you can't do something just because you're a girl."

Puzzled as to why my being a girl had anything to do with anything or why someone would stop me, I tucked that bit of information away in my brain. "You can do anything that you put your mind to. If you want to be a doctor or a lawyer or *anything*, you just put your mind to it and you do it!"

Because of that, I learned to trust in my own judgement, make my own way in the world as a single woman. I didn't know I would spend my entire 30's and most of my 40's and 50's as a single woman, nor did I know how difficult it was to be a woman in medicine. I was by myself for 30 years. One good thing was that I could go anywhere and do anything, whenever I wanted.

~ ~ ~ ~ ~ ~ ~ ~ ~

Age 9: Sitting on the Edge of the Cave

In the summer of 1986, I was in medical school. My first husband left me alone there, and it was the first time I had ever lived without someone else in the house with me. Most other students went home or on an extravagant vacation for their first med school summer; I missed home, so I drove back to California. But first, I visited my uncle and aunt in Nebraska, because it was so close.

Uncle Dan and Aunt Marianne had three children who stayed home all summer. My cousins Mark, Jake, and Natalie ranged from 9-12 years old, and virtually every day, Jake watched Back to the Future. They were a military family, with Uncle Dan being an officer in the Air Force. As a B-52 navigator, he was a POW in the 70s for nine months; President Nixon brought him back. We never talked about it, but every time I looked at his handsome face, I was reminded that he almost didn't survive.

Life and death oscillated with one another from one breath to another. In Anatomy class, we were continually reminded that the human body is a wondrous machine. I was beginning to cherish life more and more, not taking it for granted. I wanted to see the world.

While at their house, I needed money, so I was one of those ladies in the grocery story scooping tastes of ice cream for people to sample a new brand. Then I drove a pink ice cream truck. When there was just enough money to buy gas all the way home, I packed up to head out to Los Angeles.

And yes, it was embarrassing to work in a grocery store then drive an ice cream truck. I did it because it was the only thing to do. No one would really do that unless they needed the money.

I DROVE A
PINK
ICE CREAM
TRUCK.

No More Tears
Dr. Margaret Aranda

On the night before I left to drive back home, I woke up at 3 am and baked my cousins a nice big batch of chocolate chip cookies and hid them in a cabinet for them to find. I loved leaving a piece of myself behind, and to this day, they still remember those cookies. And that pink ice cream truck.

I drove from Tulsa to Los Angeles in a little Chevy Sprint. Once she learned I was by myself with no car, my older sister Victoria actually gifted me this red Chevy for medical school. Just like a motorcycle, it ran on 3 cylinders and got phenomenal gas mileage. There was not a real gas shortage, but I stretched my money.

In California that summer, I filed for custody of my son and hid out in a Women's Shelter for a week before driving back to medical school. My son was 9 years old, and he had a best friend named Milton. Milton was two years older than my son and he could definitely be a bit bratty, but I loved him.

I thought it would be nice for Milton to come along. So, we all drove back from Los Angeles to Tulsa, coursing along the 10 Freeway day and night. It was a long, hard drive.

Milton started asking questions.

Mountains appeared before us. In the heat of the summer, one looked to the left and then to the right. Heat waves glistened their form above the arid desert. "When are we stopping to eat?" Milton asked. We stopped to eat, and we stopped to drink. Then we had to stop so Milton could pee. Then we drove another 100 miles of flat desert as the mountains before us appeared closer and closer. Just as we passed the next mountain pass, yup, you guessed it. Another mountain pass was just in front of us. Again and again, we went through this abyss of endless road and mountain passes.

Milton was having a hard time with the drive, and it was getting more and more monotonous, irritating him. Over and over again, he asked,

"Are we there yet?" I couldn't believe it when I heard it, as my son had never asked me that question before.

"Wow," I said, "You're not actually going to keep asking me, are you?"

Well, you would have to know Milton to know what I did to stop him from asking me the same question. I figured he needed some negative reinforcement, and we were going to make a memory out of this.

Every time Milton asked,
"Are we there yet?"
I replied by popping in
an 8-track cassette that
answered,

"YOU GOTTA HAVE FAITH!"

No More Tears
Dr. Margaret Aranda

"You Gotta Have Faith."

I turned up George Michael. There were no DVDs, CDs, or movies to watch. Only music.

So, whenever Milton asked how long the drive was going to be, I simply popped in the same tape, over and over again. I loved this tape, so I just turned it up louder and louder each time it played.

"Ugh!" they said in unison.

"You are going to thank me for this when you grow up," I said, "because every time you hear George Michael, you are going to remember this trip to Carlsbad Caverns."

Through the rearview mirror, I saw them looking at one another. Shaking their heads 'no', they were certain this was endless torture, and it would never be a funny memory.

I explained that one day they would thank me for this, because instead of having an annoying memory of Milton's endless questions, they would remember the music with a smile. They didn't believe me at all, but I knew I was right.

What I didn't plan was my having the same memory whenever I hear George Michael; the reinforcement affected me, too.

Eventually, we would cross another mountain pass, and ahead of us stared another mountain pass. I would ask Milton,

"Do you have any questions to ask me?"

He and my son would answer in unison, "Nooooooo!" And we would all laugh and have great smiles and joy. And we would talk about the frontier, the cattle and the wagons that had to tread across this ground hundreds of years ago. How did they do it on foot? It was hot. It was dry. It was cold at night. The pioneers didn't have rest stops and hotel rooms, and it seemed like such a brutal walk.

To provide some relief on this unending trip, I told the boys that I would take them to Carlsbad Caverns. I had them navigate as we turned off the 10 to drive south. Little Milton was beside himself with "You Gotta Have Faith," railroaded into behaving, and as we neared the Caverns, he repeatedly started to threaten, "This better be worth it."

Again, you had to know him. My son, the ever-patient one, simply took it all in stride. He knew not to say this too often, and he better tolerated each mountain pass. But we could feel every itchiness of the two hours it took to detour to the Caverns.

We finally arrived at the Caverns, took the staircase and elevators down, down, down, and it got cooler and cooler with each step. A welcome relief from the scorching heat, soon the stalagmites and stalactites jutted out in their magnificence. Milton exclaimed, "Oh, this is so worth it!"

I just smiled.

At evening's end, an audience gathered on the edge of the cave, anticipating the bats. In a mild panic, we rushed to climb and find seats in the cement rows. The air was expectant, as it was just about time for the bats to fly out of the cave. As time progressed, the lazy sun slowly dipped down over the other side of the cliff. We waited.

Milton asked, "When are the bats coming out?"

I explained they were bats. They really don't look at a clock. They go by instinct, day and night cycles, and bat-time. He seemed to understand. We waited. And we waited . . . and you guessed it. Again, Milton asked, "When are the bats going to come out?" Peer pressure wasn't enough for Milton.

After asking three more times, at first the audience turned around to frustratingly glare at him. After a few more times, several people exclaimed, "Hush!", "Shhh!". I let it go, because at that point, the audience had more power than me.

Just then, we could hear it. My son patiently sat without speaking, trusting me on this one, too. At that very instant, I realized who my son was as a person. He was calm, reserved, patient and inconspicuous. I really liked his reactions and his demeanor; most of all, he was slow to react. He let the distractions go right over his head.

The sound continued.

Like the ripples of water at a stream, at first it was smooth and soft. As the bats neared, the enormity of their en masse wings revealed themselves. With upside-down, fluttery wings, they bounced.

Whoosh! A giant swoop echoed. Over our heads went more than a flock; it was a thousand flocks of bats! The ripples turned into a flurry that continued and continued over our heads. Just as fast as they entered, there they went! Poof!

In an instant or two they were gone, far away into the distance. Our eyes could not help but follow them as far as we could see. In another moment, the entire audience was mesmerized and silent, exhaling in one unified heave of satisfaction.

Milton looked up at me with his big, beautiful eyes, exclaiming,

"This was sooO worth it!"

I just smiled.

The rest of the whole way home, Milton never asked another question.

~ ~ ~ ~ ~ ~ ~ ~ ~ ~

My father taught me what was right and wrong. In second grade, I somehow got upset that I had one "B" on my report card. I never showed it to my mom or dad. When no one was looking, I took that little report card straight into my Dad's office. I opened his drawer and took out a pen that had a pen eraser on the top of it.

I proceeded to not only erase the "B", but to turn it into an "A." I replicated it to match the rest of my teacher's handwriting. Then I searched for my dad's signature on something. I found it. I forged his name on the "Parent's Signature" line on my report card. I turned it in to the Sister the next morning and forgot about it.

I wasn't worried about getting in trouble. I just wanted straight A's. The next evening, my dad brought me in to his office and explained to me that I had to earn my grades and that it wasn't possible to get credit for work not done. I don't think he ever told my mom because she would have been mad.

Later, my dad taught me to bowl by looking at those triangles in the floor, using it as a linear trajectory of where to aim for the ball to roll.

We had lots of books. My Aunt Mary gave us a collection of Nancy Drew Mysteries, and I liked the *Laughter is the Best Medicine* section of Reader's Digest. As I explain in my book, *Archives of the Vagina*, I learned what intercourse was from a red book my mother gave me.

The night I started my first period, I was up very late watching TV and my dad came to me, asking me what was up with my being up so late, much less watching *The Twilight Zone*.

I told my dad that I started my period and my stomach hurt.

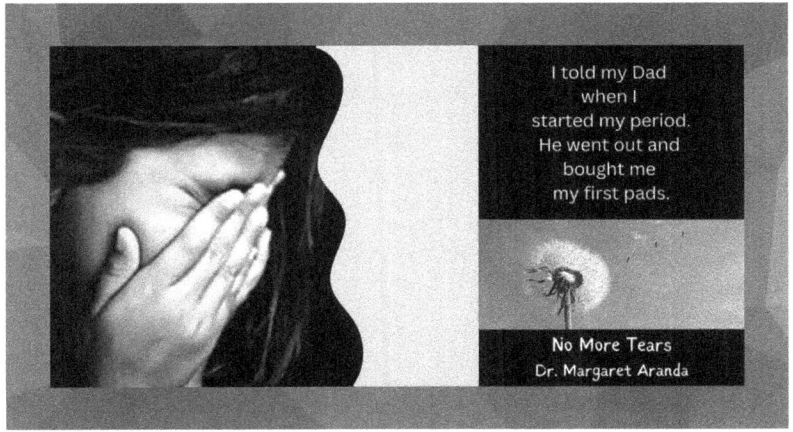

I told my Dad when I started my period. He went out and bought me my first pads.

No More Tears
Dr. Margaret Aranda

I didn't know these were "cramps," but he gently inquired more and asked me if he could do anything to help me. He found some aspirin for me, and then he went to the store and bought me my first Kotex.

After a few months, I read something about the word, "rape" but I did not know what it meant. And I couldn't figure it out from the context. I asked my dad,

"What does 'rape' mean?"

I still remember the look on his face; he was a bit irritated, but I could see his thoughts flicker. He knew it was just me, it was a genuine question, and I needed an answer. He answered,

"To force. It's something a man should never do!"

Even after going back to read that section in the book again, I was still too young to understand what that meant. I let it leave my mind, but it came back to me later, that my dad was the first person to tell me about rape.

My dad did not drink, smoke, or cuss. Maybe the worst thing I saw him do was to watch wrestling on late-night TV. As I grew to a mid-teen, he let me stay up late watching wrestling with him, but I had to leave the living room when the men started biting one another's foreheads.

As a single parent, he took custody of all seven of us kids, getting a Big Bear cabin and taking us there every weekend. He was a good dad.

Around his mid-50s, Alzheimer's came on with subtle things like being afraid of hot water in the shower or eating hot food. It graduated to forgetfulness, then wandering from the house. He got into a car accident. He was conned out of money for various sweepstakes, and became unable to manage his own finances. That's when we had to put him in a locked facility that specialized in dementia.

In the first edition of "No More Tears", I did something that many elders and patients with dementia do: I perseverated about elder abuse. I complained about it without being direct in explaining why I wanted you to be on the lookout for it, especially in a nursing home.

In this book, I can tell you what was happening.

Before the accident, my daughter was a regular visitor to her Grandpa. They walked down the nursing home hallway holding hands, and she fed him pudding. We played his favorite game, tennis, outside with him.

Then the car accident happened, and it took us away from him.

We had been randomly showing up to see Grandpa, and sometimes we would find him sitting in the shower, waiting for a towel for unknown periods of time. There were other residents: one smeared stool on the walls, another bled on the carpet, and I had to get her medical attention because they just left her like that.

I complained to everyone. I had written letters to the supervisors, the district head, and the state. Nothing helped. No one did anything and the abuse continued unabated.

Only much later did I learn there reportedly was a gang of caregivers at the facility who sequentially murdered residents. They exhumed bodies and found pillow stuffing in the respiratory tract. The last I heard, the perpetrators were on Death Row.

None of the patients could defend themselves, could express words complaining of abuse, or tell anyone what was happening. I learned that we need to take their actions and translate them into words: someone who smears stool on the walls is in pain, is suffering, and needs special help.

And when someone has a brain injury or Alzheimer's disease, they may be unable to say what they are really thinking.

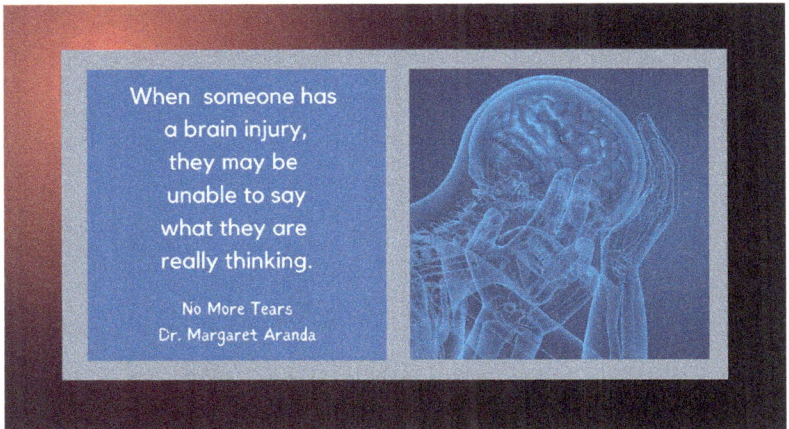

When someone has a brain injury, they may be unable to say what they are really thinking.

No More Tears
Dr. Margaret Aranda

The Car Accident

It was just another day. My daughter and I were driving back from the house we were buying to be closer to my dad. Before I put her in the car, I remember pulling on her seat belt, and then tightening it up again, to be sure there wasn't any 'give.' I did the same to our chocolate Labrador, Ella. She was in a puppy container behind my seat, so I pushed my seat back all the way so it could not be jostled.

In retrospect, maybe that was my angel or the Holy Spirit impressing on me the need to have them both be secure.

It was a Tuesday afternoon, April 2006, and it was a bright, sunshiny day in Malibu, California. A glance down at my watch showed that it was two o'clock, several hours before rush hour began. It was a perfect day to go to the beach. We had passed through Malibu Canyon, coasting to a red light in front of Pepperdine University at Pacific Coast Highway.

I remember looking off to my right to see a seagull riding the wind without flapping her wings. The baseball diamond ahead overlooked the ocean and all its glory. It was a wonderf-

CRASH! *SPIN!* CRASH AGAIN!

After spinning 360 degrees in a full circle, we faced oncoming traffic. We were stunned. No one stopped.

Finally, a man behind me got out of his car and helped me back mine off the street. It was then that I noticed a tiny BMW convertible had crashed into my driver's rear wheel, then hit a brand-new red pickup truck that was behind me. He was crushed into the huge cement telephone pole. His registration tag was still taped to his front windshield. Both he and his passenger were outside, walking.

I ran to my daughter's door, opening it with traffic buzzing past me. Everyone passed me. No one had a face. I could not see eyes, a nose, or a mouth on one single person. It was as if they were ghosts, non-humans. No one had a soul. They just whizzed by.

No one stopped.
No one had a face.
No one had a soul.
No More Tears
Dr. Margaret Aranda

I flung my daughter's door open, and it bounced back onto my arm, providing me with a nice bruise. The puppy was fine, my girl was fine, just staring at her little hand-held electronic game. Maybe that protected her? She looked up at me, just two years old, and asked me what was wrong. I don't recall my answer.

It was a very hot day, and I wasn't used to being out in the sun as I had an adversity to it. We stood out on the grass, waiting for emergency vehicles.

Finally, another man stopped and helped me get my truck to the side.

On the scene, the lady that hit me first said that she "blacked out," losing control of her car. (Later, she said she "sneezed."). I spoke to her the next morning on the phone, and she changed her story to say that she dropped some fast food on the passenger floor and when she leaned down to get it, she lost control. Instead of pressing on her brakes, she hit the gas pedal all the way to the floor.

I asked for a police report to be written, and I appreciated the assistance we all received from these trained professionals.

Seeing that only my rear bumper was slightly damaged, I volunteered (stupidly) to drive home as the other two involved cars were each towed away. In retrospect, I was not thinking clearly.

A witness walked up to me and emphatically said the lady hit us at 90 mph. He was astounded I was even standing up and made sure I was okay. She had to hit us that hard, because we spun 360 degrees to face oncoming traffic on the opposite side of the street.

In time, there were three ambulances, five CHP patrol cars, and ten CHP motorcycles. No one went away in an ambulance; there were no broken bones.

I was fine. I never hit my head. The windshield was fine.

There were no brake marks on the roadway, no dark black marks leading straight to our truck. She never used her brakes.

Everyone was fine. Everyone was walking. Or at least, everyone *seemed* fine.

They towed away her BMW and the red truck.

They told me I could drive away. No one checked my car.

Later, after talking to her lawyer, the lady that hit us would say it was "an act of God" because a bee went in her car.

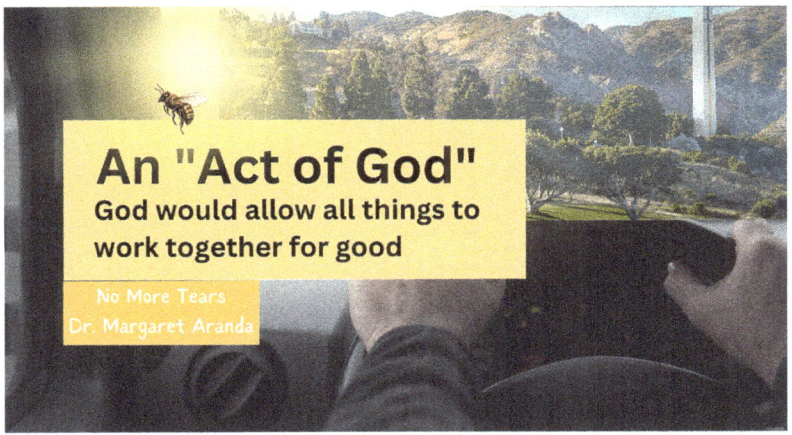

An "Act of God"
God would allow all things to
work together for good

No More Tears
Dr. Margaret Aranda

"Lady! Did You Drive that Car?"

That evening, my bridesmaid Marilyn came over for dinner. She and my husband sat at the round dinner table eating and drinking wine, while I slept on the couch. I was unable to get up. I was sleepy.

No, I was dead sleepy. Something was already starting to be wrong, but I did not know it. They didn't know it.

They drank wine and laughed the night away.

No one noticed me.

No one was home the next morning, and I had to take my car to the shop by myself, to get it checked.

I connected with the shop, and they were ready for me. I dropped off my baby with neighbors next door, people I hardly knew.

Why would I do that? Because I did not want to put her in the car. The car was a big Suburban truck, but I did not know whether it had sustained damage. Common sense told me that if she hit me first, then caused all that other damage to the red truck, which was totaled, then my truck probably had some damage.

I drove 20 miles to the shop that I trusted, following 4 different freeways. I drove 45 miles per hour. If I went faster, the truck shook and rattled.

By the time I arrived at the shop, my hands were sweaty, and I wasn't sure how I was supposed to get home.

There was a nice waiting area with signs on several exits, saying, "No Customers—Work Area." I found some coffee and nervously sat to await my verdict. I just wanted to go home.

The shop looked large and jam-packed with Porsches and Beamers that had missing or banged up parts. But the business was still small enough to be personal. It didn't smell like oil, rubber tires, or anything. Strangely enough, I recall that the bathrooms had a nice kind of air freshener that I wanted at home. I went back and sat in the waiting area.

In about 10 minutes, a shop mechanic yelled from one of the doors, "Who has the Suburban?"

I stood up, and said, "Me."

He was worried, wringing his hands. He looked me up and down. He said, "LADY! How did you get here?"

I was confused. I said,

"I drove the truck."

He told me no, I could not have driven it here.

LADY!
WHO DROVE YOU HERE?
No More Tears
Dr Margaret Aranda

I reaffirmed, assuring him that yes.

I. Actually. Drove. My. Truck. There. By. Myself.

Still in disbelief, he frustratingly said,

"*LADY!* Come here! Follow me!"

We walked past the 'No Customers' sign, outside to the shop area where the Suburban was on a lift. He leaned under the left rear, pointing with a shaking finger, and said,

"Look at that! Your rear axle is *broken! How could you drive here?*"

I didn't even know what an axle was, but I saw the cylinder holding both rear tires. It was broken in half. *In half.*

I was dumbfounded. I took a step back, and said,

"I don't know. Maybe my angels were protecting me . . ."

But reality was setting in.

It was a *bad accident.*

As he took his blue cap off and rubbed his forehead, he said that the rear axle was broken. The entire thing could have cracked upon my drive there, and *voilà*! I would have been in yet another accident.

Brotman Auto Body drove me to the local Enterprise, where I rented a car and then drove home.

I spent the next three days constantly sleeping. It was like being drugged with sleeping pills.

And so that explains how hard the hit was, as well as my subsequent injuries sustained by a large torque spinning force that spun my brain and ripped an artery going up my neck to the back of my brain.

As it turns out, my pituitary gland hit the hard ventricle of my brain, knocking out my ability to hold on to water, something that is incompatible with life.

From then on, I was in and out of emergency rooms.

Eventually, I would not be able to walk or talk.

A Place with "No More Tears"

I know what I am talking about because I felt heaven.

Hum drum. Cross your fingers or tie a bow around one finger and remember that throughout this book, I live drip to drip (intravenous fluid) and battery to battery (nine volts, to be specific). The "Hum, drum" is my pump, pumping in fluid 24-7 so that my heart does not empty of fluid, so I can stand up without fainting (syncope). The "Drip, drop" is intravenous fluid that gave me a blood pressure, brain function, and life. They run continuously through this book.

They were tired of me at the ER. No one knew what was wrong with me. They literally rolled their eyes at me as if to say, "We don't know what is wrong with her. Why does she keep coming in?"

It was my twenty-third visit. They looked at me as if I was faking it. It was as if the car accident occurred, and then I was bedridden.

This time, it was different. Instead of leaving me in the ER, they literally took me to the second floor and put me in a room by myself. No nurse. No monitors. By myself.

That's when he walked in, as if it was just another day.

He was wearing a black shirt that had a white collar in the middle, and black pants. He gently carried a small glass jar with salad oil in it. Only there was no salad. No one was eating.

What was he going to do? I blinked, closing my eyes for a moment.

He was quietly on my right side, leaning over me. I don't remember any words or questions. He dipped a finger in the oil, began praying, and then raised his arm to touch my forehead.

I closed my eyes.

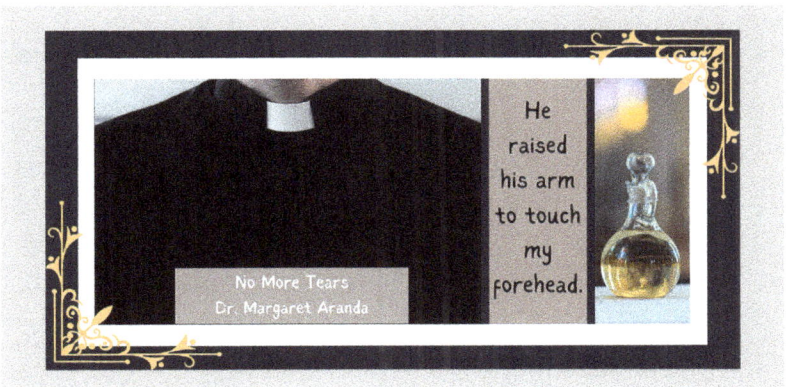

When I opened them, huger-than-life iridescent bubbles gleefully bounced before me, on my right, in groups of two or three. They were larger than a person. There were some bubbles traveling alone, but most were in groups. It was as if someone was blowing child's bubbles behind me, and instead of straying away randomly, the bubbles honed-in on a central and elongated tunnel of sorts. The bubbles hopped along ahead of me toward a bright light, a door. That's when it hit me.

Whoosh!

I felt the overwhelming "*No more tears.*"

Stop. Stop. Try to feel this place. Sh . . . sh . . . shh . . . Close your eyes for one minute. Now. Feel this place.

As I turned, I was drenched in this place, this moment. I was in a place with "no more tears." I would never cry again. I would never shed a tear. No sadness, no misery. No pain.

I remember feeling the awesomeness of this 'no more tears' feeling. It covered me like water in a tub; it lifted me up in my soul.

Simultaneously, I remember saying to myself, most passionately, *"Don't cry for me."*

I thought of my daughter and son, my family. If they *knew* how happy I was, how happy I would be *for all eternity,* they would not cry for me. They would *have a party!* They would wish they were with me. They would have joy and look forward to meeting me here when they too pass to this world.

Here I was, outside the door to heaven. I was filled with profound relief and ecstatic joy at never crying again. I felt it so purely and so overwhelmingly that I hope to impart on you one iota of what it feels like to have "no more tears."

And to impress upon you an indelible story that will change your individual human world forever. To let you know that you too can really, truly be at heaven's door and be possessed with the monumental knowledge that you would have "no more tears" for all eternity. To feel "no more tears" and revel and bask in the enormity of an eternity of it. Unimaginable.

You are bathed (i.e., submersed, surrounded, uplifted, and glowing) with one immediate trait of knowledge: no more tears.

I simultaneously comprehended that my most beloved ones on earth would be crying for me forever, either literally or in their own memories. I knew that I lay in the emergency room gurney with death's mask on my face, pale and green with blue veins under my eyes.

No one ever told me about this place.

I had been there at the moment of death for many of my ICU patients. I was there as each person took his or her last breath, "gave up the spirit," and died. Some died with a smile, a peaceful smile on their faces, their eyes glancing into the distance. Others breathed heavily for hours or days, suffering through it but eventually, the spirit left the body.

I then tried to rest on the knowledge that my daughter would grow up without me guiding her through life, laughing with her, playing with her hair, or tucking her into bed. My grown son would never talk to me again. I knew that my family loved ones would not see me again. I would never again share a Christmas gathering with them.

All these thoughts were in a constant stream.

Then the "no more tears" came back, a stunning knowledge and self-realization that I vehemently and most assuredly said to myself,

"They are crying for me on earth. But I am not crying for them."

I would never, ever shed one more tear that rolled down my cheek and landed on the floor. My eyes would never fill with tears again. Why, they would never cry one single tear!

It was as if I opened my eyes again, and suddenly, God was before my left as a great sun, shining. He bounded and pulsated with a slow, deep masculine hum. Boom. Boom. Masculine, deep. *Love. Pure love.*

I had no sin, no judgement. If I did, it was far away and out of sight and memory. I was pure.

"To be absent from the body is to be present with the Lord."

Just pure. Love. Bounding. From my wonderful God who loved me like I was the only girl in creation. It was just him and me. No one else.

I tried to look at God, in the core, the very middle of his being. But it burned my eyes.

I tried
to
Look at God

No More Tears
Dr. Margaret Aranda

When it started *really* burning, I tried to keep looking at his core, somehow thinking I would see his face, his shape. But the pain got sharp, very sharp and I was afraid I would be blinded. So, I moved my eyes to the right. But a thought danced in my head as I remembered . . .

Moses. He was blinded by the same light.

I looked down at the silhouette of my body, floating in outer space without tone. The stars and constellations were around us, beautiful and vast in their enormous expansion.

My ankles and wrists hung downward, limp. I floated with the outline of my body sort of invisible. I could see its outline in white light, but my core was see-through. I could see the constellations through the middle of my legs and arms. My eyes gazed at the silhouette of my right leg for a moment longer.

I continued turning to my right. I noticed his light warming the right side of my leg, and I wondered,

"Why didn't his light touch my left leg, the closer leg? It's physically closer."

The light went upward, through my whole body, and up to my head. It was warm and nonpainful.

I was still caught up in the mathematical puzzle of how God's light missed my left leg and went straight to my right leg. I recall kicking myself a bit for being preoccupied with the physics of the place and reminded myself that God wasn't supposed to follow earth's rules. He could follow whatever rules he wanted.

That's when I looked up and saw the stairway. It was not just Led Zeppelin's stairway; it was

THE *STAIRWAY TO HEAVEN.*

The Stairway to Heaven

I looked to my right. I saw the blue planet earth in the distance, very small and very far away. There were clouds surrounding it, just like in every picture.

I turned to my left. I was at the bottom of the stairway. The stairway was magnificent and bold white. While very wide at the bottom, it gracefully curved upward, sloping with smaller and smaller stairs. There was a gigantic puffy white cumulous cloud at the top, extending laterally beyond the staircase, but not by far. God spoke without words, saying,

"You can go up."

GOD SAID, "YOU CAN GO UP."

No More Tears
Dr. Margaret Aranda

I did what he told me to do, and my body floated up to the bottom of the right stairway, near the chunky edge of the curved and pedestaled railing. Passing the curved rail at the bottom right of the stairs, I floated up the right side. My wrists and ankles continued to dangle. When I got to the top, I paused, floating.

The cloud was tall and wide, extremely bright white but not blinding, as God had been. The cloud was of the cumulous variety, fluffy and billowing out gracefully to encompass the top of the stairs.

When I arrived at the top stair, I suspended myself and noted there was a gap of outer space between the top step and the cloud. I could see millions of stars in the darkness of space. It was as if one had to jump from the top step, over the gap, to get inside the cloud. It took my breath away, but I had no fear.

For a fleeting moment, I thought that if I missed the distance jumping into the cloud, I could fall into outer space from between the top stair and the cloud.

I looked back at Earth, which was in the far distance to my right, as if to bid it adieu, to say goodbye.

Through E.S.P., God again spoke four words,

"You can go in."

**GOD SAID,
"YOU CAN GO IN."**

No More Tears
Dr. Margaret Aranda

I was overcome. I had to make a decision.

I turned to him. I turned to the cloud. I saw my father running towards me, *so happy* I had arrived! He was pitched forward, wearing pants and a shirt, and his arms swung from side to side near his chest. Both hands were in a fist because he was running so rapidly, toward me. I felt his excitement and joy!

I looked at him, taking him in. I felt him. I smelled his scent, so I knew it was really him.

But I hesitated and looked back and forth. I stayed at the top step. I didn't go in. Something was stopping me.

Again, I turned to my right, to planet Earth. It was small and off to my right, in the distance.

I couldn't do it. I couldn't take that last step.

I couldn't go in, not now. I was overcome by wanting to be there for my daughter. She was only two years old.

I COULDN'T GO IN, NOT NOW.

No More Tears
Dr. Margaret Aranda

I took one step back and bowed in humility to God. I remember feeling like I wanted to crawl under a rock and hide.

I felt ungrateful and unworthy.

The words were silent, yet the words were said as if they were spoken. They were hesitant, a bit trepid.

"I know it is my time. And I thank you that I know where I am going when I die. I know I get to go to heaven. But . . . if . . . it . . . is . . . okay . . . with . . . you, . . . I would like to watch my daughter grow up."

I was more than pensive, hesitant to request anything of him, my majestic God who let me feel the 'no more tears' of his presence, his heaven. Words rolled out of my mind in spurts, searching for the right words, the right sentiments.

Then, the words came as a pure flood, unashamedly flowing in a long and uninterrupted trail, as if they were contained in the middle of tears.

I switched from asking to begging. I begged him. I mean, with a heavy heart, *I deeply begged God to let me stay on earth.*

"Please God, take everything I ever did that was good, all the times I made dinner for my sisters, all the sandwiches I made, all the laundry, and all the times I stayed up late with patients I didn't have to lose sleep over. Remember the kid in the jail ward who lied about his age? I made him promise me to get new friends and make something out of his life. I didn't sleep. I stayed up with him.

Please, please take everything I ever did . . . and make it count for good, make it add up to let me go back to my little girl and watch her grow up. Please, God . . ."

I begged him.

I felt ungrateful and very small. I felt like a child.

I closed my eyes.

I gave myself to his mercy.

In doing so, I bent my spiritual silhouette forward, as if to bow to my Lord and my God. Nothing happened.

I waited. Nothing happened.

And then I opened my eyes.

When I opened my eyes, I could feel the priest taking his thumb off my forehead. So long ago when he came into my room, it was holy oil in that bottle, my Last Rights. He had made the sign of the cross in about five seconds, saying,

"I bless you in the name of the Father and of the Son, and of the Holy Spirit."

And my vision, the stairway to heaven and my conversations with God . . . all that detail happened in those five seconds.

What I Learned

People ask me if I told the priest what happened, where I went, and that I stood before God and the stairway to heaven. I was too sick. At that time, I thought it was a dream, and I was in a state of near disbelief.

It was as if the near-death experience had to wear off a bit for the carnal world to sink into my presence. Like a postictal seizure, I was still under its spell, numb and unaware of what transpired.

I learned that God has a different time frame than we do. That is exactly why he wants us to exercise patience.

I learned I'm going to heaven for all eternity. And the best news is that if you want to be with your maker and not separated from his love, he provided a ticket that is free to us: we only need to accept his Son, our Lord Jesus Christ, into our heart and confess him as the Son of God.

I not only realized that God listens to us, but that he cares about our happiness, our well-being, and our wishes and deepest desires.

I was supposed to die, but he let me come back.

Instead of taking everything I did to let me *go to heaven*, i.e., by works, he took everything I did and let me go *back to earth*. Or maybe not . . . maybe he just wanted to give me the desires of my heart, and my begging was my limp effort to think I needed to persuade him when he had already granted my wish.

I was supposed to die right then, but he changed my future and let me exercise my own free will to come back to earth.

God is God. So, he simply *changed my destiny*. All things were new.

God wants us to be happy. I begged him to go back to earth, but I don't think I had to beg.

Like Dorothy in the Wizard of Oz, all I had to do was ask. Instead of clicking my heels three times, he would have granted my wish.

And if he did it for me, he will do it for you.

Unlike the God I was raised with in elementary school, the God I met was persuaded by me. He acquiesced to my desires, my passionate pleas and gave me what I wanted.

Like any parent, if we beg him for something, he will give it to us if he sees the passion! Why? Because he knows our heart, our intentions. But like our parents, they already know what we want before we ask. And many parents cannot stand to have their kids beg, so maybe God granted me my wish before I even started begging.

I learned that what I do in the future does not impact what God does for me now. None of these things mattered: my promises, goals, dedication, plans, or future intentions to do anything for him.

What did matter to God is my past, my track record. What I did, how I served others and served him, the promises I already kept, my dedication already shown, the plans I followed through on for his purposes, and my past intentions filled by my actions.

He believed me. He knew me. He loved me with pure love.

He knew he could count on me. And as far as the east is from the west, he separated tears from my mind. God expelled all flickers of sadness, sin, or wrongdoings; they would never even become a thought.

God separated tears from my mind

No More Tears
Dr. Margaret Aranda

Getting Worse before Getting Better

It took my faith in God, perseverance, my own medical knowledge, and "doctor shopping" to ultimately reach a long list of diagnoses.

To reach a point in my life where I could stand up and walk, I had to micromanage myself as a physician and think as a physician.

Soon, my daughter was six. She never knew when an ambulance would be in our driveway, or when her mommy would be taken to the hospital. She did not know if her Mommy would be home when she got home from school, or if she would be up to help her get ready to go in the morning.

Deep down, she never knew if this would be the time that Mommy never came home. Or if she would die.

Every time I came home from the hospital, I had to teach her to trust in loving me again. I was a stranger and repeatedly, she forgot who I was.

She wasn't used to having me around.

Then I would roll on the bed with her screaming and punching her tiny fists on me, and I would say, "You're my Missy! And my Bissy! You're the most wonderful girl in the world! Mommy loves you! Mommy needs you! Mamma's home, babies!"

Both exhausted and sweaty, we would finally fall asleep in one another's arms. She would have her tiny hand on one of my ears, caressing it.

She would say, "Mommy! It's you! Mommy, I missed you! I love you!"

As time would eventually tell, only I was injured in the accident.

My neighborhood mothers volunteered to me that I was plodding around because I "took" all the injuries the same way as any good mother would want it to be so that my child would have none.

Months later, I lay in my bed upstairs. Something was very wrong with me, and I felt death was upon me, slowing taking my soul away.

Unbeknownst to me, my left vertebral artery had begun to dissect. I looked out the leaded glass windows to the pepper trees and oleanders beyond, thinking that I would never get to garden again.

I looked around our room, focusing on the bedroom set that we picked out after being newly married. It was a good bed to die in. If I fell asleep, I knew I would not wake up. I was tired.

I don't know why I didn't telephone my husband who was downstairs. Instead, I reached for the phone in a last-ditch effort to relay my thoughts.

I called my sister Cathy in Maine, barely able to whisper my sentiments. I told her that I felt that I was going to die. I said, "Make sure and promise me that my daughter will always be in touch with your daughter. I want all my clothes to go to my daughter, and my son and husband could figure out the rest."

I didn't have the energy to say much else other than,

"I feel like I'm about to die" and "I love you forever."

I didn't really believe it, or I would have called my husband. I just felt so tired.

My eyes watered, and the tears dropped over my nose as I waited for the inevitable deep sleep to overcome me and take me away. I was ready to rest. To let my soul go.

My sister apparently was upset as we hung up. Immediately, she began stewing, wondering whether to contact my husband. After twenty minutes, she called him.

He immediately raced up the two flights of wooden stairs to reach me. Suddenly, I was being pushed and prodded. I could hear his voice in the distance, but I couldn't turn over. He turned me over and later said that I had the "look of death" on my face.

As doctors, we both knew what that meant. He asked me to confirm whether I called my sister, telling her I felt like I was going to die. I confirmed it.

He asked me if I wanted to go to the emergency room. I was too tired to think. I was too tired to speak. I said nothing.

He took control. By taking control and stopping what he was doing, he saved my life. If he hadn't taken me to the ER, I would have died alone in bed, probably within minutes.

I had no diagnoses. No one yet knew I even had a traumatic brain injury, much less a vertebral artery dissection, dysautonomia, gastroparesis and a neurogenic bladder.

Our nanny rounded up supplies. The house turned into a hornet's nest of determination and deadlines, and to the emergency room we went. Maybe we should have called an ambulance; we'll never know.

My cousin, who happened to be staying at our home, held my hand the whole way to the hospital. I made her promise to take a year off to be a nanny for our daughter if I died. She agreed and she kept me talking, which sequentially kept me breathing, which by God's grace helped molecules of oxygen go to my brain.

I am convinced that this most assuredly left me with less of a brain injury than I otherwise could have sustained. Flashing forward in time among other things, I did end up with two small strokes in my midbrain.

The midbrain, particularly a place called the pons, contains centers for such basic bodily functions as respiration, blood pressure regulation, heart rate regulation, and vomiting. It is a different area of a traditional stroke in the outside curly cerebrum brain that leaves people unable to talk or walk on one side or smile on one side.

Instead, this was a stroke that made my heart rate and blood pressure so unregulated and disjointed that I would faint just by standing up.

I presented to the emergency room with a chief complaint of "Feeling like I am about to die."

No one *ever* says that.

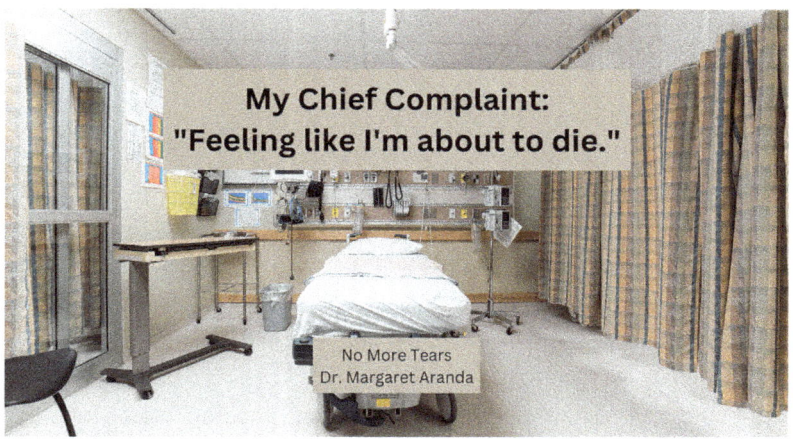

I don't think there's a medical billing (ICD-10) code for that presentation. Goodness knows what they thought of me, but it must have been scary for any doctor to hear any patient say that.

That should have been a 'red flag.'

Instead, they left me unattended. They called a Catholic priest who came to my right side, opened a glass jar of oil, and dipped his fingers with it.

You know the rest of my near-death experience.

I am less inclined to hold back my tears of joy because someday I will have no more tears.

While you can, revel in your own tears of joy. Because in heaven, there are no more tears ever again. I've felt it, the no more tears. It is not possible for there to be anything like it here on planet earth. It is not here. It is in heaven.

Every time I reread this chapter, I am dissatisfied. There is no way for me to explain the things that I saw at the door of heaven. It is as if written words cannot truly convey the enormity of this to you. I come back again and again to read this chapter, and my description falls far short.

I felt the rays of light from heaven touching my feet. I felt the warmth of pure joy, the peace that passes all understanding, and the sense of being in flight.

To be absent from the body is to be present with the Lord.

In one blink of the eye, there was the outer space, the stairway to heaven itself, and the planet earth behind me. I know the Psalms teach us the Lord is our shepherd and we shall not want.

We should be content with whatever we have, for virtually whatever situation we are in. If we can learn from it, we can grow from it.

~ ~ ~ ~ ~ ~ ~ ~ ~ ~

Age 13: Everything Just So

It was another weekend to make thirty-five sandwiches, so seven kids could have one sandwich a day for the school week. My father had custody of all seven of us, and my mom was mostly gone. They had separate bedrooms and my mom came home every other weekend, so we regularly got to see her. This was a great scenario, because we got to stay in the same house and grow up together almost like nothing bad ever happened.

I swiped mayonnaise on another piece of bread, then took a mental image of the kitchen table, round and covered with a Thanksgiving tablecloth. It was another Sunday afternoon. Turkey leftovers were stripped, the bones were bare, and little pieces of turkey dotted another sandwich.

I had five sisters and one brother; I was the second oldest. No one really 'made' me do it, but I liked to cook and bake. Naturally, I had to make sandwiches for school, which was less than two blocks away from home. We lived in a former convent for Catholic nuns, and it was as if the goodness from the nuns still hung around the house.

Turkey meat dotted a casserole dish here and there, and I separated the dark meat from the white meat. I inquired of each child which they preferred. No, that was not even possible in a large family.

Living in a big family means that you get what you get, and if you don't want it, someone else is looking up with big eyes to eat if for you. I didn't know that dark meat tasted different than white meat, so I just mixed them both up on the same sandwich. None of my siblings would notice, either.

I opened the freezer. Thirty-five sandwiches, to be exact. They were all lined up, one sandwich per day for five days of school. I was finished!

Peering down at the kitchen floor, I noted the laudry piles: red, white, and blue. And another one for mixed patterns. I dumped the dryer, then loaded the washer with the printed clothes, and added the detergent and softener to the machine. I knew to use cold water on the permanent press, and certainly and of course, I knew one had to add bleach to the white clothes. Looking at the piles, I calculate there were three more hours of laundry for nine people.

I took the load from the dryer and placed it on the living room sofa. Folding each item was rather nice because it was cold and the wind was howling outside, leaves splashing onto the front steps for me to sweep on another day. In sharp contrast, the clothes were warm and soft, mildly scented. Mostly, they were warm. It was a side effect that on this cold Fall day, the clothes came out of the dryer and the warmth massaged and comforted my soul.

I placed nine stacks of clothes on the top of the sofa, on the head rest. Starting from the littlest one, each pile contained one person's clothes. Pants went on the bottom of the pile, then shirts, then socks and underwear.

I rolled socks up by matching pair, making sure that the exact sock had its own pair. I knew that depending on where the socks had been, even one white sock could differ from another white sock, and my dad's blue calf socks had to be matched just so. I did it without complaining, and I did it every week for three years, until I left home at sixteen.

Finally, I put the last socks on top of the last pile, and then it was my time. I brushed my teeth, washed my face, and brushed my hair. Then I took a nice warm and long shower. We had plenty of warm water and we never ran out of it. There was always a water shortage, but my dad never made us take quick showers.

Exiting the shower and getting in clean pajamas, I swiped back my bedsheets and blankets. There was nothing and no one that could take away my ability to lay down at night.

I gathered three pieces of my favorite snack, plain white bread. I picked up my Nancy Drew book, wondering what the next chapter would bring. Settling in, I finally had my own time to myself. I was tired but pleasantly pooped, and no one could take this time away.

It was mine.

I put my head on a pillow as the light of the moon cast its glow.

It was my turn now.

~ ~ ~ ~ ~ ~ ~ ~ ~

The light of the moon cast its glow

No More Tears
Dr. Margaret Aranda

I know that God leads us "through the valley of the shadow of death" and leads us to still waters.

Shadows don't hurt us. It was as if a mild but strong magnet into heaven was pulling me, but I was not ready to leave earth.

I trusted God for each moment, each smile from my family's face, each hum of the hummingbirds that clustered around my leaded glass window seat.

Hum drum, drip, drop.

God allowed for a seemingly predestined life to not follow the predicted pattern of simple fate but to deviate from statistics by showing me that mere humans can trigger actions or pleas that create a domino effect that leads to change God's mind.

A human and a group of humans in prayer were able to influence God so that life and miracles could occur. It allowed me to pass on what I have learned, to give you hope and inspiration, exercises, and bodily strength to recuperate after a life-changing event has occurred.

I am not special. You too can live for God and lay your life down on the floor before him, most humbly.

But do not just go to God when you need him or when you want something. You should have such a good relationship with him that God makes things happen for you.

I have asked for a sign from God many, many times when I really needed to know he was holding me in his arms.

You probably do not have to think about walking around after sitting in a chair. You just get up and walk without any conscious effort as to your motions. For me, there was an exceeding amount of energy spent in doing such seemingly simple tasks. I changed positions with conscious effort, and I walked with every step being deliberate.

God considered my request to live. The enormity of this still makes me feel so small, yet important to God.

God never failed me.

A PICC Line

Hum drum and Drip, Drop.

My IV peripherally inserted central catheter (PICC) line was my life. I had to remember to change my battery before falling asleep for the night; otherwise, I would shuffle in the dark to accomplish this task.

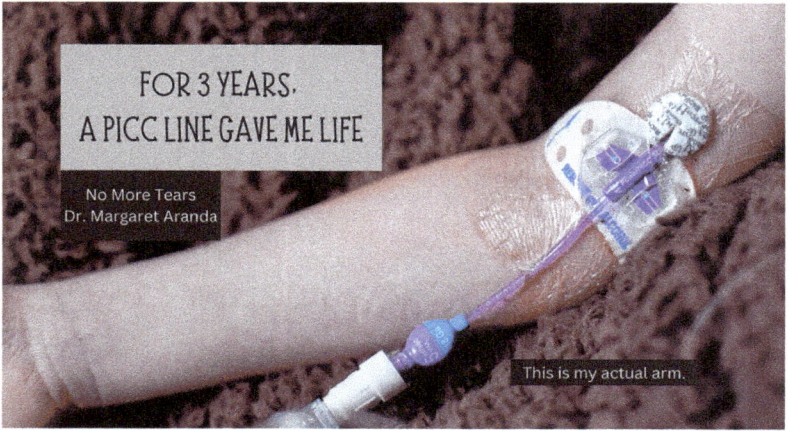

FOR 3 YEARS,
A PICC LINE GAVE ME LIFE

No More Tears
Dr. Margaret Aranda

This is my actual arm.

This is my actual arm, around 2007.

For three years, a PICC line gave me life. I both loved and hated its eternal *Drip, Drop* and *Hum, Drum.*

Lots of times, I forgot or denied to myself that I even had this IV. I would just get up and walk away from my bag.

Usually, I figured out that I left it behind when I felt a "twang" of the IV line or when I heard the Camelback that houses all the IV content. It usually fell to the ground, but on a rare occasion it would pull the line out a bit.

It's hard to take a shower with an IV in your arm. You can't get it wet, or it will become infected. Shampooing my hair takes on a whole different meaning and feeling the beads of warm water run down my back is a simple but delightful pleasure.

Don't leave home without an extra IV bag and extra batteries; you never know if there's going to be an earthquake or a traffic jam. Because if the IV stops, it clots and then it doesn't work. If the IV stops working, it could mean your life.

It seems that every three months, my central IV line was infected. Time after time, I made it out of hospitalizations, and when I got home, I was like a petri dish just waiting for another central line infection.

There went another hospitalization, perhaps 40 per year. My PICC line(s) needed changing from the left arm to the right arm or vice versa every three months for almost a couple of years now.

They told me I needed this fluid for the rest of my life. I did not accept it. My peripherally inserted central catheter (PICC) IV-line pumps in sugar water at 65 cc/hr.

Statistically and increasing with time going by, one could see that one day there will be no veins left. And I did not want a line in my neck or my chest.

One weekend, a nurse had me alone in the radiology suite under fluoro. The left arm PICC was extremely difficult to glide across the chest to my heart. It kept getting stuck, bending on a vein. At one point, it went up the wrong way and I could feel it banging on my left forehead. I thought I was going to die on the table. That's the day I vowed to go off the IV. I started at 64 cc/hr. The next day, I went down to 63 cc/hr. Eventually, I was down to 20 cc/hour and then they took it out.

It was one of the best days of my life.

Perseverance

Each morning that I opened my eyes, I would slowly realize that I was still alive. Before the thrill of it got away with me, I slowed down and became conscious of my consciousness. I felt my neurons fire as the brain's reticular activating system awakened tens then hundreds of thousands of neurons.

Being in touch with gradual awakening was a skill that made me appreciate the morning flickers of life.

In the original book written over ten years ago, I took you straight to the car accident. I didn't do that for effect. I did it because I was unable to recall much of my previous life memories.

In this book, I gave you time to know me.

In those first ten years, I called my caregiver for every little thing I needed. I constantly knocked on the wall. If something fell, or if I fell, I was stuck, and I could not get up.

Giving up was not an option. But of course, I was so disabled that the thought of dying gave me pause.

⌐ ⌐ ⌐ ⌐ ⌐ ⌐ ⌐ ⌐ ⌐ ⌐

Age 14: Too Young to Know

At age fourteen, I left the solstice and serenity of elementary school to go to a private high school. We had red and black plaid uniforms with pleats all around the skirt; the white shirts boasted rounded collars and short sleeves. I wore Wallabees and bobby socks.

On the weekends, I still made 35 sandwiches for 7 kids, and did laundry for nine. Five days a week, I made a full breakfast for everyone, loaded and started the dishwasher.

The only thing I didn't do was make dinner; my mom did that. But on the weekends, I learned how to sauté onions, brown ground beef, cook lasagna noodles, and make lasagna. I knew how to make a pot of pinto beans and cook up some great-smelling Mexican rice.

By the time I was 15, I tired of everything. I had no one my age to talk to. All my friends had two parents, and mine were getting a divorce. They lived in separate rooms in the house, and my mom left on the weekends. Clearly, she had her own life, and she was living it.

There was no such thing as a counselor at school that you could talk to, so I started smoking cigarettes.

During First Period, Andrea and I snuck out to meet in the Girl's Room. We sat and talked about sex, life, and the parts of our life that were missing.

Andrea was one year older than me, already had sex with boys.

I wanted to learn from her so that I could learn what older boys were like. She told colored stories about traveling on the back of a biker's motorcycle, wearing regular clothes on the weekends, and her parents who mysteriously let her do everything and go everywhere.

My stories were fantastically boring and dry. I revealed my home situation. After telling her about my siblings, we gratefully moved on to more refreshing topics: music, movies, and makeup. And boys.

And of course, we talked about sex. We did not discuss real sex, just kissing, holding hands, and feeling a boy's arms around you.

Andrea lived a freestyle and carefree life. With all my grown-up responsibilities, I was fascinatingly enamored by her surreal hitch-hiking adventures. All her friends rode motorcycles wherever they wanted and stayed up until the sun rose.

I didn't know if she was lying or telling the truth about her stories. Nonetheless, they solidified my belief there was an outside world containing smiles, laughter, childishness, dancing, frolicking, and well, just happiness: no people yelling at one another, no fights, no pulling hair, no screaming, no nothing. Just peace.

We smoked our cigarettes and never got caught. Same time, same place, just like Batman. The weekends went by. For once, I looked forward to Mondays because her escapades consistently opened new doors.

But one Monday arrived and I rushed to meet her; she wasn't there to smoke a cigarette. I didn't buy smokes, so I didn't have a cigarette that day. I went along with my day, not thinking too much about her.

"She must be sick," I thought. "I'll just catch her tomorrow."

Another day went by. Again, she wasn't there. I didn't have her home phone number because I only saw her at school. Unknown to me, her classroom desk was ominously empty, too. The other kids didn't like her too much; she did not fit in with them. Her absence did not make a mark, and everyone went on with their days.

On day three, morning school line-up time ended, the sharp bell rang, and they announced that they were taking us into the Chapel.

Hmm. Ok.

That was different. The entire school proceeded to move as a crowded group. We nonchalantly chatted, rather excited for the change. As we made our way up the stairs this cloudy day, our cheeks welcomed mist-speckled, minute droplets that spoke of promised afternoon rain.

With navy blue sweaters pulled tight, we scooted indoors, rubbed our hands, and greeted the warm Chapel heater. At the pew entrance, we dipped our fingers in Holy Water and made the sign of the cross on our foreheads, whispering, "In the name of the Father, and the Son, and the Holy Spirit. Amen."

In our innocence, we failed to note the conspicuous significance of spicy incense that gently bellowed upward.

As the speaker made his way to the pulpit, we got ready to be bored to tears and develop instantaneous narcolepsy.

We grossly miscalculated the scenario.

With slow and deliberate words, he announced that Andrea died. They told us. The System, the Church, the School, the Grown-ups, the Establishment. They told us that she was dead. This was their way of doing it.

"She is never coming back," I thought. "I was her best friend."

What happened?

She had been thumbing. She regularly hitch-hiked, I knew this. I knew all her stories. Well, someone picked her up on a motorcycle was all they knew. It was almost like they were telling us it was her fault for thumbing a ride, coming awfully close to telling us that it was her own fault or that she somehow deserved it.

Bits and pieces of information stunned me. I didn't know how to process or comprehend her death, who to think of right now, who to go to. No one offered grief counseling; there was none of that.

I swallowed. She would never meet me in the Girl's Room. I would never see her smile again. She couldn't tell any more stories of the glories of her adventures. I wouldn't see her lips suck on a cigarette, nor watch as she flicked the ashes with her index finger pointed just so.

I already missed her. The man's words faded into an abyss, then continued to roll out, louder now and seemingly angry. Yes, he was angry, and it was making me angry, too.

I looked to my right and to my left. They weren't my friends, not like Andrea.

In the distance, the man drawled, "Gun shot. Gun shot in the head."

The words echoed louder and louder and I didn't know where anyone would get a gun. They found her body on the side of a road, rolled over into a rocky ditch.

That's what he said. In a ditch on the side of the road with a gun shot in her head.

I cried.

It happened too fast. The Funeral was tomorrow. In a blur, the Funeral was now.

Now I was sitting in the same Chapel with the same man, the same voice, the same group of people. Only now it was more crowded, more rain, more incense. Everyone was wearing black.

We said goodbye to Andrea that day, I said goodbye to Andrea that day, and I felt guilty that I was still alive.

It wasn't fair. This never should have happened to her, and she deserved a long life. Now, she was never coming back. She would never have a 'long' kiss with a boy, where their tongues touched, nor would her hair jump in the wild wind as she nestled on the back of a motorcycle.

I would wake up and go to sleep and wake up and go to sleep and wake up and go to sleep and she would never, ever, ever, ever wake up again and she would never, ever, ever go to sleep again and never, ever, ever would I ever, ever, ever see her smile or ever, ever, ever hear her laughter or ever, ever, ever see her lips curl over her beautiful teeth while she laughed so softly, so beautifully.

Never. Ever. And for all eternity.

I was too young to grasp. Too young to know what was happening, what had happened. I never got counseling, and the school never talked about her again.

The big unwritten message was that if we thumbed a ride and left our parents on the weekends, we would end up dead with a bullet in our head and our body in some remote and ugly ditch somewhere, and it would be an awful way to die, and our body would just be lying there for days, and no one would even know whose body it was.

I blinked when the audience stood up in unison. The Funeral was over, and the classes began to file out of the church. Usually, we exited one pew row at a time. Today, everyone wanted to escape.

The gigantic doors of the Chapel opened.

"Let me Out!"

My insides screamed an unending scream.

In unison, both church doors opened, and the sun cracked its stream of yellow light into the Chapel. The stream turned into a door.

At first, we filed out slowly. But as the sun enveloped us with its enormity and warmth, we ran. Something was still inside us that we searched to escape. We all did it at once, and together.

We ran away from the Chapel and into the light.

~ ~ ~ ~ ~ ~ ~ ~ ~ ~

After Andrea and through my youth, I was not exposed to death. My paternal grandmother passed away when I was about thirty. My Uncle David and Aunt Barbara had passed away after being married for over fifty years. He was an ordained Lutheran minister who influenced my spirituality in many ways, reading the Bible to me as a child and bringing God into every conversation.

Because of my Uncle David, 'perseverance' developed another meaning for me, aside from achieving goals. It encompassed

Godfulness. It reminded me to get through one day, to realize God is in charge.

I had no choice but to persevere. But determination and a strong will were not enough. I had to believe not only in myself but in *why* God has me on planet earth.

I couldn't take "no" for an answer.

I had to make things happen, but at the same time, I had no power to 'make' thing happen. God could do much more than me.

What did God want me to learn? What was it that allowed the freak accident to nearly kill me? And why did I survive?

I had to be the best person I could be.

I had to love the people I was tempted to hate, or it would turn me into a different person, one that was 'less' than my best person.

I am responsible and accountable to God the Father for every misconduct I witness, for every morsel of inequity, for my decisions, for my actions and especially, for my *lack of action*.

I cannot and should not turn my head the other way when it comes to my being apprised of spousal abuse, child abuse, incest, molestation, rape, and murder or iniquities inflicted upon the poor, the innocent, or the vulnerable.

Man is inherently evil.

> *"All that is necessary for evil to triumph is for good men to do nothing."* ~ Edmund Burke

I was to live as perfectly as possible, with an ultimate awareness of my awakening. Each day, each minute of life brought the newness of God's creation in me.

One more day was one more chance.

> My life was to be lived as perfectly as possible,
> with an ultimate awareness of my awakening,
> and all that each day brought to my mind.

God in My Life

God's hand is in my life, as it is in your life.

We know this because the Bible tells us that he is no respecter of persons . . . What he does for one, he will do for all. I figured that if he could make a blind man see, he could heal my brain. That's also because the nerve fibers in the eye go into the brain and are more like brain tissue than eye tissue.

If he can make a blind man see, he can heal anything.

Live an aware life. Let unexpected happenings be a message from God. Perfection is not found in a perfect manicure—sometimes, it is found with dirt under the fingernails that tell tales of God's goodness.

Recognize that in order to be a parent, you must put God first, then yourself. Otherwise, you won't and can't be there for your family.

Live each day fighting for what is right before God, despite whoever hates you for it.

These are the things I have learned, but it's not just me. It's also those that have had repeated hospitalizations and complications of a long-term state of illness.

We are survivors of adversity that surrounds us, statistics that are stacked up against us, and professional opinions that contribute nothing to our well-being.

We must constantly fight our own desire to just curl up in bed and stay there.

We do whatever we can do. We sit up, we stand up, and we go. We brush our teeth if we can, or we just chew on a piece of gum.

We take life a little slower and go to bed at night praying for insight, forgiveness, and another day. We wake up in the morning, and before opening our eyes, we appreciate the sunrise and the birds chirping before us.

Being eternally grateful for another day and all the possibilities that one day can encompass with faith in God, we take one day at a time. We cherish each moment, each memory.

Constantly listen to your body and don't think you are going crazy because the doctors cannot figure out your diagnosis.

Visit doctor after doctor after doctor until someone knows someone who is the expert in the field who runs specialized tests and provides you with the diagnosis, prognosis, and the planned treatment.

Go on with life and live it.

Travel with your intravenous line in.

Travel by day or by night, by car or by plane.

Spread the joy that you cannot contain in your head. You must share joy with others.

Speak life into your life.

See yourself well, growing nerves, growing new organs.

Persevere.

Here is a man I have never forgotten, who made himself a lasting story in my life.

I carried my IV bag in my backpack as I entered an aquarium store. I just needed a net. There. One of the workers looked at me, traced his eyes down to my IV, and made a couple comments.

"What are you doing out of bed with an IV? You need to go back home and lay down."

My answer? With determination on my face and irritation going through my brain, I smiled,

"I have a life to live and a family to be a part of. Stay in the hospital?" "Ha! I just got out! I went to Chicago last week, and no one is going to take my life away from me."

In shock, the gentleman replied now in splendor, "You go, girl! Wow! You are a real trooper." Made my day.

You can be a trooper, too.

If I hadn't been faced with repeated obstacles in life, I would not have learned to persevere. If I hadn't learned to persevere, I would not have survived.

What I thought was a curse or bad luck, God laid in front of me to build my faith. What God laid in front of me to build my faith, was my ticket back to earth.

~ ~ ~ ~ ~ ~ ~ ~ ~

Age 30: Graduating and Being on the Bottom

My son saw me through the grueling nature of medical school. He made his first grilled cheese sandwich when he was seven, and when I was in medical school, he was such a lovie. He carried the laundry to the laundromat, and helped with home chores so I could sleep.

I am sorry that he grew up so fast. He screamed when he had to go to preschool; I had started college. He was happy to move back to California in my third year of medical school, then he saw me crying on the way home from USC residency.

There's no other way to say this but to explain that the department was hard on women. I never let on to the program or to any residents that I was a single parent with no child support or alimony. No one knew that on weekends, I cleaned toilets at a law office for grocery money. I never complained, never let on. When my car broke down or the transmission went out, no one helped me. The stupid car shops constantly milked me for money, and I still don't like talking to them.

My Dad helped babysit, my sisters helped, and my beautiful son Rueben was my precious "lovie". As he grew up, he was much taller than me, and waiters would think we were at a restaurant on a date, not mother:son. We both felt that we grew up together, because we did.

I was 19 when I had him, and 42 when I had my daughter. Through both separations and divorces, my children would both be taken away from me by their fathers. I would spend dreadful years suffering without them.

After Rueben begged me to quit medical school for years, now it was four days before medical school graduation.

If my son hadn't been the sweet angel that he was, I would not have been able to finish medical school while raising him. Nor would I have completed internship, residency, or Fellowship.

He was my everything.

Once, on a Saturday morning while in medical school, I had to go on rounds to see all the patients with our Attending. I had to take my son with me, because I didn't want to leave him at home alone. When my Team realized the situation, one doctor took off his lab coat and let him wear it, then introduced him to every patient as "Dr. Doogie Howser". We sure had a blast that day!

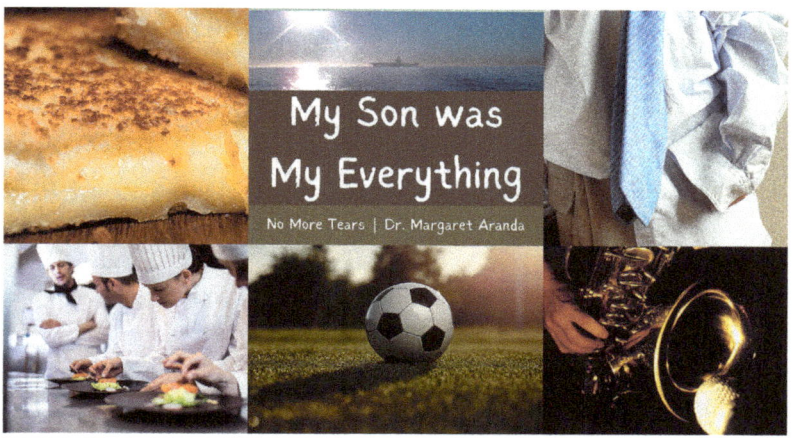

Four days before medical school, here I was, asking my son again,

"Is it okay with you if I go to medical school?"

He said, "Well, since you only have 4 days left, it's okay. I guess."

I had tried to engage him in my escapades, but clearly he was too young. I was getting ready to do the impossible, to finish what no one thought could be done, to complete that which seemed to be just out of my grasp. And he barely was proud of this feat.

I repeated not only my entire first year of medical school, but there was a little 'catch' of sorts when I transferred from Oral Roberts' University Medical School to USC School of Medicine. All my core rotations had to be repeated at USC. I ended up doing everything twice: Surgery, Internal Medicine, Pediatrics, Ob/Gyn, Cardiology, etc. This not only made me learn everything twice but allowed my breadth of knowledge to expand to two institutions and their idiosyncrasies. This widened scope made me a better doctor.

So, I graduated.

On graduation morning, I awoke to a dozen red roses from Frank, a trucker friend who helped me get home when I left ORU in Oklahoma. I sat in the blistering heat and at the end of the ceremony, they told us we could throw our graduation caps in the air.

My first thought was, "But it's rented. I must return it."

At that moment, I looked up. Thousands and billions of hats jostled upward in God's sky, twisting and turning any way they wanted to go.

I wanted mine to be one of them.

I threw my hat as far up in the air as I could, thinking the stupid rental company must be used to us all turning in different sizes when we go back to their store!

And I laughed with gleeful jubilance!

No one could ever take this away from me. No one. Ever.

Later, after we hugged and cried, I tried to gather my cap from the ground, tears of joy streamed down my face, because finally, finally, finally, I graduated medical school.

Woot ~ Woot!

It was done!

It was 1990, I was 30 years old, and I was on top of the world.

I was accepted into Anesthesiology Residency at USC, and was to start my Internship at USC, also. A year of Transitional Medicine through the Internal Medicine program awaited me, and it would prepare me to be an anesthesiologist.

I looked forward to it all.

"How could internship possibly be THAT hard?" I thought.

It was one year long. 365 days. I could do it.

I graduated, I took a week off, and then I was on the bottom of the ladder again, as an Intern.

I knew I would be up early in the morning, and up late at night.

I would be working weekends and holidays.

If I missed Thanksgiving with my family, I would 'get' Christmas. If I was off on Christmas, I had to work both Christmas Eve and New Year's Day.

I was at the bottom of the lowest rung on the ladder.

All the "scut work" went to me: not just drawing blood but stamping every label and walking every tube to the correct lab. It meant wheeling patients to Radiology for an x-ray. I was a secretary, transporter, and delivery person. The only thing I did not have to do was empty the trash.

My first day of Internship occurred on a memorably hot July morning in 1990. Having literally drawn the short straw in a contest of seventy interns, my assignment led me straight to the 13th Floor of big County Hospital. In a heat wave. With no air conditioning. To Jail Ward.

Jail Ward Orientation was at 0700 sharp.

An elderly and stout woman with gray hair, Dr. Osborne, calmly described the "Locked-Down Policy."

She said, "You have all drawn straws to be here. This is LA County Jail Ward. Welcome to The Beast."

She proceeded to instruct us not to leave a pen in the wrong place. A patient could try to stab us in the neck with it. If any of the jail patients took one of us hostage, there was a full Lock-Down Policy. The huge

6-inch steel door entry to the Jail Ward would close, the key would turn; no one was getting in, and no one was getting out.

We would stay.

We looked at one another turning green in the face, and we vowed to watch out for one another.

Gulp.

My first patient was an 18-year-old African American male who reportedly tried to shoot his girlfriend. The LAPD shot him fourteen times, and he was paralyzed from the waist down.

He cried every morning when he saw me.

He hated getting his blood drawn, and of course that was the first thing that I had to do. The only way I could make it better for both of us was to do it as fast and as painlessly as I possibly could.

And I wondered.

Did I go to medical school for this? To have an attempted murderer as my patient? I had no idea how he survived all those bullets, and this was the first time I witnessed a miraculous escape from certain death.

I struggled with the ethics of it all. Daily, I struggled with it.

Finally, on the third day, I gave in to my double training, stopped fighting the ethical dilemma, and accepted my fate as his doctor.

Contrary to popular thought, not every doctor takes the Hippocratic Oath. I took the original Hippocratic Oath, not a modification or a different oath. My USC graduating Class of 1990 was given a choice of which oath we wanted to take:

1. *The original Hippocratic oath;*
2. *A modified Hippocratic Oath (i.e., we could add, delete, or hange it);*
3. *An original oath of our own making.*

My USC Class of 1990 voted to take the original oath. I would do my best to "do no harm."

So, every morning for a month, that great heavy steel door closed on me and Lisa Hayworth, MD, as we Interned on the Jail Ward for our first rotation in medical school.

We also left that place at 7 pm, watching as we turned our heads in unison to listen to that huge door shut itself behind us at the end of another day.

We counted the days 31, 30, 29 . . . 3, 2, 1.

And finally, we made it out of jail.

~ ~ ~ ~ ~ ~ ~ ~ ~

Making Mistakes

Intentional or not, stupid or not, mistakes are forgivable.

After graduating high school by testing out and receiving a certificate legally equivalent to a high school diploma in any California college, I ran away. I was sixteen years old.

I started junior college that same year, but then came down with chicken pox and was out of college for three years before going back. I didn't know about dropping classes, and my Political Science teacher gave me an earned "F."

After years of exemption requests the teacher denied, I was able to get an "Administrative Change" that changed the "F" to a "Withdraw."

If that "F" had remained on my transcript, I never would have had the GPA to enter medical school.

Maybe God had me thinking about changing my report card way back when I was seven years old? Maybe I grew up thinking I needed straight "A"s and I would or could not settle for less.

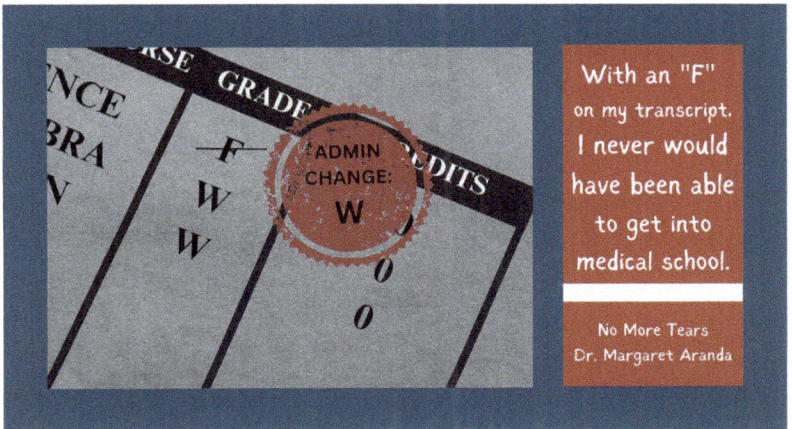

With an "F" on my transcript. I never would have been able to get into medical school.

No More Tears
Dr. Margaret Aranda

And it was a good thing I went to medical school, or else I don't think that I would be alive.

Who could have known that it would take a doctor to save a doctor?

I believe God granted me the ability to return to earth and be a messenger to you. He not only wants you to be in the crowd of individuals that believe in him, but he wants you to live your life for him.

When we accept Christ into our hearts as our personal Savior, we die to ourselves and become alive to Christ. It does not stop there.

"No one goes to the Father, except through the Son."

Once we have died to ourselves and have become alive for Christ, we must seek his face and listen for that small still voice of the Holy Spirit that he left us with (Christ did not want to leave us alone, so he sent us the Holy Spirit). He has a plan for your life. It is laid out before you, and you do not even know where it will lead you.

Don't tell me that you don't have a reason for living. You do. Just because you feel alone, that does not mean that you are alone. You are never alone. Your reason for living cannot be found within yourself. It can only be found when you live for Christ.

Besides waking up every day to live for the evening, and then going to sleep every night waiting for the daytime, I died to myself every day. I died to myself every minute, and every hour.

And sometimes, as the saying goes, you have to live one day at a time. That wasn't good enough for me, because I thought literally each day, that I was going to die. One day was too long for me to think about.

Instead of taking one day at a time, there were many days that I took *one hour at a time.*

Gratitude

I think those bubbles going before me were filled with intercessory prayers. I was an ordained minister and held Sunday Bible Study for children in South Africa (see Appendix), also supporting an orphanage. The bubbles happily danced before me, leading the way to my Lord.

At that time, I thanked God for each morning and for each evening, literally.

People ask, "How did you do it? How did you spend twelve years in bed?"

I lived 12 hours at a time. At sunrise, I longed to live until sunset. And at sunset, my goal was to be alive in the morning.

I lived sunrise to sunset, then sunset to sunrise.

No More Tears
Dr. Margaret Aranda

Day after day, month after month, and year after year, I lived 12 hours at a time. Eventually, the 12 hours became twelve years.

I realized I was a living a synthetic miracle, and I was grateful for medical technology. I wore a tiny gray Camelback backpack that my son picked out for me. I modified it with a button to hold an intravenous bag and a pump. It went with me everywhere; I could not live without it. It pumped fluid into my arm and if it stopped, the line would clot, and it would be a monstrous ordeal to un-clot it or to try to put another one in.

I was grateful to have survived that awful PICC line ordeal. But there is a bit more to the story.

Age 47: Death by PICC Line Catheter

On the scariest occasion, a nurse had me in the basement radiology suite at the hospital. It was a Saturday and no one else was there but us. I was on a blood thinner, Plavix, because my neck artery had an aneurysm, and it was at high risk to clot. If that catheter went anywhere it was not supposed to go, it could pop right through a vein. Then I would bleed to death.

Instead of weeding in correctly, it had gone from my left arm under the collar bone, to the left internal jugular vein, and up to the left side my brain. She advanced it with a push, push, that went, "Punch! Punch!" inside my left forehead.

Barely moving to speak, I begged her to stop. She did.

I was so scared one of those punches was going to make me bleed to death that I held my breath as the catheter finally pushed its way across my chest, to the right upper heart chamber area.

That day, I almost died on that x-ray table. That was the day I swore to get off that PICC line.

I was so grateful to not be dead on the table, that I pulled off a white gold, antique diamond ring from my finger. I gave it to her for saving my life, for getting me the heck out of that room!

I wanted that stupid PICC line out of my arm, and I never wanted to have another one again. And I am grateful that I got my wish.

But the radiologists wanted to go into my neck veins. My life looked like it was destined to be just as long as my arm veins lasted, as long as the PICC line lasted. It pumped fluid into my heart, 24/7. That was no way to live, and I was going to get off that stupid PICC line! I still had my spunk, and no one could take that away from me.

I was grateful to live second to second, knowing that any minute I could fall and have a blood clot go to my brain on the one hand, or a brain bleed on the other hand.

Was I going to clot, or was I going to bleed?

Each minute, each hour that went by was an accomplishment. I held on to every moment. If I could move my toes, I moved them. But for the most part, I stared at the ceiling, being bedridden.

The years in a wheelchair were challenging; the wheelchair was much less of a problem than the actual living.

But when I changed from a lying to sitting to standing position, I got light-headed or flat out fainted.

Most of the time, I was unable to do even that; I had to crawl on the floor because I was unable to stand. I surely couldn't walk unless I held on to someone or something, bent forward like an old witch, so that my head was lower than my heart.

I still couldn't speak well. I first had to formulate what I was going to say in my head, then mentally put the words together, then start speaking. Slowly. My brain words always came faster than my speech, and if they came too fast, my speech stuttered, the words mixed up, and I frustratingly had to start over again.

I was grateful that after three years, I went from a wheelchair to a walker. I didn't want to fall. I was gripped by the constant fear of falling, of bleeding, of hitting my head again. To put myself at ease, on one hospitalization I stole a "Falling Precautions" sign from my wall, and took it home.

"Don't Fall!"

Below that, it said,

"Call for Help before Getting Up!"

I took it home because it justified my asking for help. And asking for help wasn't a luxury; it was an unwelcomed necessity.

After three years in a walker, I was grateful to go from a walker to a cane. I could speak better; I even held a book signing at my house (see Appendix). I had to sit in my walker a lot. It wasn't possible for me to mingle or go here and there; everyone had to come to me.

Initially, I felt the benefits of walking with a cane far outweighed the risk of a falling injury. But after three years, I almost tripped and fell on the cane. So, I threw it away. I felt the benefits of walking with a cane were far outweighed by the risk of a falling injury.

I was grateful that the minutes stretched out so that by the time I was better, I looked back.

Sometimes, someone was with me. Most of the time, I was alone. At times I was in my own bed, but a lot of the time, I was in a hospital bed. Sometimes that hospital bed was in the ER, lined up with a bunch of other patients and beeping noises everywhere; other times, I had a roommate or on a good admission, I had a private room.

I could move, but I spent a lot of time on my back. Obviously, I wanted to see the world and I spent time ministering on the internet, gained a lot of friends on social media, and started writing.

People helped the time pass. And eventually, my time was served, and I could exist like other people.

When it was all over, I had been bedridden for twelve years.

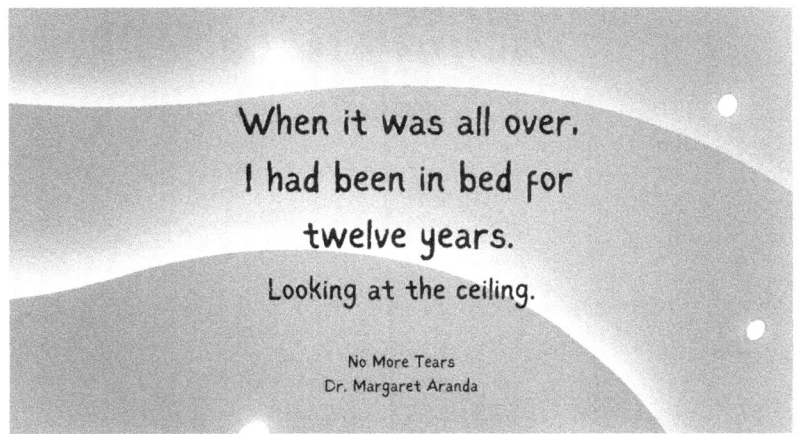

When it was all over,
I had been in bed for
twelve years.
Looking at the ceiling.

No More Tears
Dr. Margaret Aranda

Twelve. Years.

With God, time was different.

Twelve years went by in the blink of an eye.

At the same time, one blink of an eye lasted twelve years.

When I woke up, everyone was gray.

How Did I Do It?

People ask me all the time . . . "How did you do it?"

As they ask, people think about how they would spend twelve disabled years in bed. They search for my secret.

How did I go on for one more day? How did 'one more day' stretch out into twelve years in bed?

Life for me has been reflective indeed.

You must know that everything you've been through has made you who you are. If you suffered, that brought you to understand suffering. It made you a better person more willing and able to help the next suffering person.

Because of my suffering, I know exactly what to say to someone in my position.

For example, I suffered two miscarriages. Now, most people haven't had a miscarriage. So, most people don't know what to say to a woman who just lost her baby. But they want to help.

When I had my miscarriages, here are common things people said:

"It was probably going to die anyway."

"There was probably something wrong with it."

"It probably had bad genes."

You can see how none of those help, right? They can make an already sad person feel even sadder, like . . .

"Wow, now there's something wrong with my genes, too? "

"I was feeling bad, but now I feel worse."

"It wasn't an 'it.' It was a baby."

After a miscarriage, here are some good things to say:

"I'm sorry. I don't know what to say."

"I don't know what that feels like, but I am sure sorry for your loss."

"I had one too. You definitely go through a lot of hormone changes, right?"

At the last comment, the woman looks up at me, instead of down at the floor, to say, "How did you know? You mean I'm not the only one with such mixed-up emotions?" She smiles because she feels the same way I did.

And now, suddenly, she no longer feels alone.

You see that if you know pain, you know what to say to the next person. That's why God gave us one another.

I got through twelve years in bed just moments at a time. When I was going through those times, they seemed fiercely difficult. But now, looking back, you know what?

Twelve years really went by in the blink of an eye. It was a gradual recovery, but it was as if suddenly, I could stand up, I could walk. I could speak, I could move better.

How did I do it?

I kept persevering. I kept praying, I saw myself better. I died to myself every day. I spoke life into my life. I read the Bible, I taught the Bible, I lived for God.

I saw myself well. I spoke not the things that were. I spoke that which was about to be. I saw myself getting out of that wheelchair and swimming again, walking again.

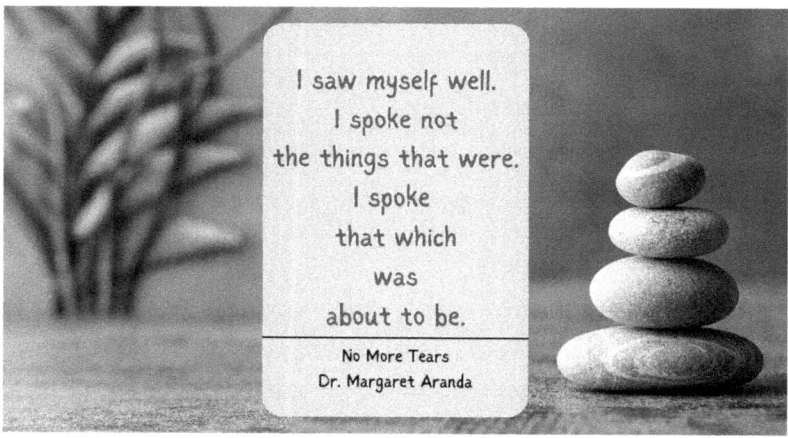

I saw myself well.
I spoke not
the things that were.
I spoke
that which
was
about to be.

No More Tears
Dr. Margaret Aranda

I gave up my concept of time, whether it be months, hours, minutes, or moments. I waited on God.

Not only did I wait, but I stopped asking God for anything specific. I let him recreate me, reinvent me, do what he wanted.

I let all the revenge, all the sorrow, and all the pain go to him. I looked at my problems like they were a tiny speckle on the wall of a Grand Canyon rock, surrounded by the earth, the solar system, and the universe.

When I pray, I usually don't ask something specific. My continual prayer to God is, "Open the doors that need to be opened and close the doors that need to be closed."

I trust him to be the Great God that turns the negative into the positive. Only he was the Creator, the One to cause not only my physical miracles, but to command any other miracles to be manifested in my life.

I didn't even ask for my daughter back. Instead, I saw myself with her.

I did not ask God to punish my ex-husband who left me. I gave that to God.

I never even asked for my career back.

In fact, there was a day when I was cleaning out my closet and I happened upon my doctor's white coat. I reached past denial and cried, clutching at it and not yet ready to admit my career was over. My thoughts descended through the next stage of loss, anger.

I threw my lab coat away. I knew it was gone.

Now, twelve years had passed. I spontaneously started buying dress clothes and shoes. I took all my Continuing Medical Education (CME) and updated my medical license. Unsure of where it would go, I had no plans to look for a position, nor did I know how to start a medical practice.

But I trusted God.

I knew God would answer my prayers *in more ways than I would have known to ask or even to pray for.*

I knew God could give me more than what I could think or dream. And I knew that he *would.*

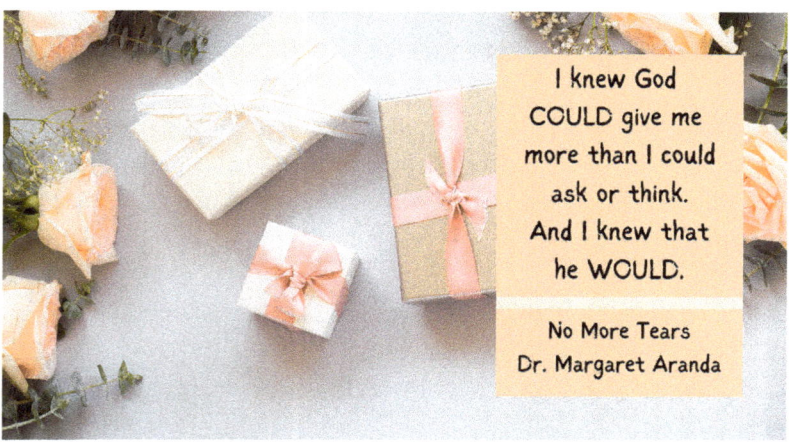

I knew God COULD give me more than I could ask or think. And I knew that he WOULD.

No More Tears
Dr. Margaret Aranda

Age 51: Gray

I turned on the television.

Everyone was gray.

Being Able

When you are disabled for a decade, you can forget about some of the things you used to do. It's almost like a resignation, because the struggle to survive must go on and one door needs to close before another opens.

Because my brain was so affected by the injury, I tried to do the things I knew I loved to do. This is when I started writing. It was a mechanism to save my mind. In recollecting and reminiscing, I felt that I was preserving the salvageable pieces of my mind.

The power and capabilities of the human body always intrigued me.

Age 6: Walking on Water

At age six, I walked across an indoor pool area.

It was humid, and the air smelled like chlorine.

There was a young lady with a white rubber swim cap snapped under her chin. The words "9 Feet" were written on the wall just behind her head. I was walking behind my sister, but when I started staring at the lady, I had to hold on to my sister.

I was really staring. I couldn't figure it out.

I carefully turned to look at the number "9" on the wall, then incredulously looked at her outstretched arms scuttling water in nine feet of water!

I thought,

"How was she standing up in 9 feet of water? Were her feet touching the bottom of the pool?"

It was magic.

Fascinated, I vowed that I too would learn to do the same thing, to walk on the water.

Every summer we were booked at the local pool. I went from a polliwog to a dolphin and loved the smell of chlorine on my skin after swimming at Northridge Pool.

Because we were volunteer Junior Lifeguards, we got to stay inside the swimming area during lunchtime, when it was closed to the public. Then we would stay past closing time, to do Swim Team.

All seven of us kids spent the entire summer days at the park. We did water ballet and our team continually qualified for local competitions. One year, we came in third for all-city water ballet.

I went to Granada Hills High School, now Granada Hills Charter, which embarrassingly did not allow its unvaccinated students to attend their outdoor graduation ceremony. It was particularly upsetting that of those not allowed to attend, seven were students with special needs.

I would walk from Northridge to Granada Hills for school, then walk to Petit Park a couple miles away, then do swim team, then walk all the way home and do my homework.

I would push myself to do more laps for years on end, swimming up to 1,000 meters per day, five to seven days a week. It would take me an hour to swim. No matter what exams came up, I swam for an hour straight, rain or shine, even if it snowed.

During one lunchtime workout during medical school, a man tapped on my head as I began to do a flip turn. He was the Swim Team Coach at ORU. He said I was a good swimmer and asked me to be on the swim team! I had to say no because I had to spend so much time studying. But it was a feather in my cap, a big compliment.

Running was my second favorite sport. I loved the smell of a freshly cut grass in the morning air as I used my determination to push myself to run harder and faster (2.5-mile course including hills; seventeen minutes was my best time). I continued running through medical school at ORU, where we had to pass a fitness test each semester, for

"Mind, Body and Spirit."

ORU: Mind, Body and Spirit.
No More Tears | Dr. Margaret Aranda

I joined racquetball intramurals on the medical school team that played against the undergraduates. My father taught me how to play racquetball, so I played hard. My serves always got me at least one point for our team, as I made them land in a back corner, very close to the ground. No one knew whether to move forward and hit my serve before it landed, or to wait until it landed. My arm was strong, and the ball's force was great. We came in third place.

Age 27: Arranging Our Schedules

Rueben and I ate at the same restaurant, Vito's, for pizza every Friday night. It was right across the street from ORU, and we walked.

I didn't have much money, so I would buy the all-you-can-eat salad bar for $2.99 and Rueben would get two pieces of pizza for the same price. We took our bottomless cups, so drinks were free. Rueben would save me his pizza crust, and then he would play PacMan for 25 cents. No matter what happened, or what test I had coming up, we kept our "date", and as a single parent, this was super important to both of us.

When I was On Call overnight, obviously I could not pick him up from school, so at age 7, someone different would pick him up, take him home, and then take him to school the next day, rain or shine. Or snow. We both worried that someone would forget about him, but no one ever did. The wives of my medical school class organized this for me, and it was a lifesaver.

But after a while, and of course, it wore on him. That's when someone spoke to the medical school for me, paving my way to transfer and go back home for help raising Rueben.

On that final day before driving back to Los Angeles, Rueben had me stop by Vito's Pizza, so we could go there one more time. We both knew we would never be back.

It was very bittersweet. Somehow, we knew that the bad days would be remembered as good days.

We were in tears.

During Critical Care Fellowship, I went to the gym a lot. I couldn't fit in a swimming pool, so I ran on Stanford campus. I loved to dance on the weekends, alternating between night clubs and the Top of the Drake, the Sir Francis Drake Hotel in downtown San Francisco.

At the University of Pennsylvania, I swam again. Linda and I ran the school track and ventured long cross-country runs along country roads in Bucks County.

Once we ran so far on a hot day that I was seeing black with white spots, and we stopped at a local church. They were in service, but Linda wanted to ask for water. We were dripping sweat and wearing shorts while all the churchgoers were dressed for the Lord. They were super responsive, treated us like their children, and gave us ice cold water! That was the best tasting water I have ever had.

All this to say that I grew up athletic, I loved moving my body, and I was determined to get my body back. I also struggled to get my brain back, but writing a book helped. By the time I finished a book, I hated it for all the effort it took. But I did wrote and edited six books in twelve years, over and over again. I knew it would be good for me.

That's why I moved my body in bed. I developed bed exercises (see Appendix) because no one really taught me how to exercise in bed. I couldn't go swimming, but I could move in bed.

Today in the post-COVID era, we have many bedridden people who suffer with the same dysautonomia that afflicted me for so many years. Imagine how awful it is to be unable to stand up, to be sentenced to being bedridden, just because our bodies do not want to function on planet earth.

Now that I have recovered, I believe that health is one of the richest things a person can own. But in order, here are my top three important things in life that no one can take away from you:

4. God
5. Your health
6. Your education

If you know God, you will never lose him. If you lose God in your life, you must find him again. If you don't even know him enough to talk to him every day, then you need to know him.

If you lose your health, you must try to get it back.

No one can lose their education. It is in your soul, in your spirit.

TRAVELING

I am fortunate to have traveled and it is something important to my quality of life. When I was disabled, it saddened and depressed me to miss any opportunity to travel.

In the final analysis, it occurred to me that I could be sick "here or there," so I may as well be sick "there."

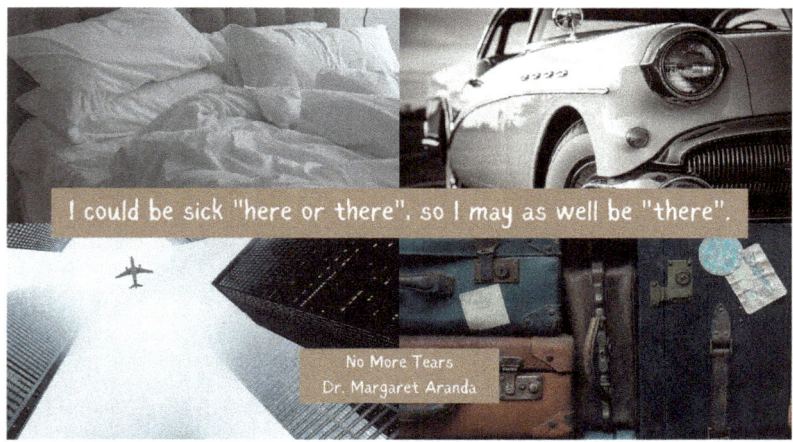

As a child, we moved to and from Texas, so a road trip and travel trailer were familiar. As we traveled in the car, I passed the time by drawing pictures of mountains and horses. It made me feel very calm and serene.

Age 13: Wild Raspberries in Alaska

I was thirteen and my parents were letting me fly to Alaska by myself, to visit my best friend from kindergarten, Angela.

It was my first big trip away from home. The summer air was dry and I took a few sweaters because I figured Alaska must be cold.

Her mom was a real mom, and Anchorage, Alaska was beautiful.

We went on road trips with her parents and brother, and their dog Dandi went everywhere with us.

On drives, we stopped to pick wild raspberries from the side of the road. I never made jam before, but that was what we were going to do.

We saw ice glaciers, wild moose, and mountain goats. The mountains reflected into the lakes and ponds before them, and if you looked closely, you couldn't tell which was the mountain, and which was the reflection.

Her brother and father were funny, and I had never seen a father: son interaction. They delivered papers, folding them up every morning on the living room floor, and counting their collected money each week. I had never seen so much cash, so I figured they must be rich.

My parents weren't like their parents, and it was an experience of a lifetime to be with "a real family." I loved them all and felt like part of the family.

Angela's brother also had a friend staying at the same time, and he traveled from California with a broken leg.

We took him everywhere with his crutches, up the mountain side and down the mountain side. Slowly.

He was a good sport.

In the back lot was a trail, and we were entrusted to ride motorcycles up and down the hills. It was a fantasy life for me, as with seven children in our family, each one of us never seemed to get as much attention as kids did in this home.

On car trips, Dandi would fart in the car so bad we had to air it out by opening all the windows.

Somehow, Dandi knew she stunk up the car, and her eyes would look at us with "The Look of Shame" which made us laugh all the more!

It's that same look that dogs get when they wear those big plastic protectors over their head, so they don't bite or scratch at a wound.

"That Look of Shame" is the funniest self-realization a dog can attain.

So many great memories we had together. I cried and cried the night before I left Alaska, wishing I could stay and live with their family.

That was one of the best summers of my life.

On the plane back, I didn't feel like a real person. I was in the sky and in a cloud on a piece of metal with 'No Smoking' signs.

But I knew what I was leaving behind, and it was a good thing.

The only remnant I brought home with me was a jar of homemade jam. And what a FINE jar it was!

There is nothing like homemade.

Years later, during my time of disability, I lost the friendship with Angela, and I'll never know why. I'm sure I said something out of context because back then, thoughts would just go to my lips and then come out.

I lost her, but I hope she comes back to me one day. The loss of this friendship still bothers me.

In high school, there were four of us that lived within walking distance, and we did everything together. On one occasion, I went to the beach with Eileen's family. Two memorable things happened:

1) We ate lobster at this huge campfire her father made (I had never seen live ones boiled); and
2) When no one was looking, we snuck into the men's showers.

The line to the women's shower was just too long, and we couldn't wait.

It was Eileen's idea to sneak into the men's, and I was the conservative rule-follower, so I initially didn't want to do it.

Then I thought it would be a change to be daring . . .

But we forgot to think about *how we would get out of there* once we were done.

Eileen and I finally ran out with a towel draped over our heads (thank goodness we each had 2 towels!).

Boy, the comments we got!

I travelled to Tulsa, Oklahoma, for ORU Medical School (married and with my child). At ORU, I was the first medical student woman to go through a divorce.

Some felt I should stay in medical school because that is where God wanted me. Others felt I should quit medical school and go back home to the man who beat and abused me. They didn't know, and I didn't want to tell them.

I cried.

I studied through my tears.

He took our son back to California with him, and I cried some more.

I cried so much that I had to repeat my first year of medical school, but it was a good thing. I ended up knowing everything twice as well, and I earned good grades.

Age 29: Quitting Medical School

My son cried every day, every night.

My soul ripped and I eventually could not eat or sleep.

One of the senior medical students saw me sitting at a desk, in a classroom on the Holy Spirit. She stayed after everyone left and asked me what was wrong.

I didn't know she could tell something was wrong. But apparently my eyes were sunken in, I only weighed about 100 pounds, and I was dragging.

By the end of a short conversation, she knew my heart. She told me to leave my books on the light brown wooden desk, then to follow her. At my questioning face, she assured me that surely no one would steal my books, so I let her take me by the hand.

Down the bright hallway we went, and I did not know that I would never see her again. She took me to the Dean of the Medical School's office and told me to wait outside.

I waited while they talked, feeling worried. I didn't want to get kicked out of medical school.

I was a single parent. I was the first to go through a breakup, and I hadn't yet filed for divorce.

My hands were beginning to sweat.

After an endless time, they both came out, and she left without a word. Not one word.

I didn't know what she told him. I thought maybe my life was over.

The Dean sat me down and came to me like a fatherly man. He said,

"I think you are having too much trouble in medical school, being a single parent. Do you think your family can help you take care of your son?"

I said, "Why, I think so . . . Yes! Of course, they will help me."

He said,

"Come back tomorrow to see me at 9 am. I'll have something waiting for you."

I could hardly sleep.

The next morning, I was outside his office thirty minutes early.

He opened the big brown glossy door with his name on it. Then he stepped inside and gave me a deep bow, motioning me to go in.

I went in and sat on a soft brown leather chair. Everything was brown.

He handed me a tall yellow manilla envelope.

It wasn't too thick. It wasn't heavy. I looked at the front and there was no name, no address, no writing on the front.

Before I looked at the back, I hesitatingly looked up at him. He gently said,

"Go ahead and open it."

It was unsealed. I slowly turned it over and carefully pulled out a neat set of papers.

On the top page was a gold seal, and a letter with his signature on it. I read the letter.

I started crying.

Attached were my medical school transcripts, an official copy.

The introduction letter continued, saying not only that the transcripts were official, but that the medical school was releasing me to pursue entrance and acceptance into a medical school closer to my home in California.

They were letting me go.

I was incredulous. What about all my stuff? How was I going to move? I didn't even have a place to go, or a school to transfer into!

My sister Judy flew out to Tulsa, and we packed up whatever could fit in my car: medical school books, clothes, some sentimental things—and that Letter.

Much later, I did have a friend that helped me move boxes of things to California, for free.

I left my apartment full of furniture.

We crammed my belongings into my 3-cylinder Sprint that my sister Katrina had given me as a medical school gift. I never saw my furniture again.

Because I needed family help caring for my son, we moved to Los Angeles. I was filing for a divorce and going on with my life.

I picked up the phone on a day that it snowed in Northridge. I had gone out to breakfast, and then it snowed! It had been 30 years since anyone had seen it snow in town, and the cars were slipping on the streets.

I finally got home. I decided to make two phone calls: one to UCLA and the other to USC.

I called UCLA first. When I told them what happened, and the letter I had in my hand, they said,

"We don't have a spot for you."

So I hung up.

I took a deep breath and immediately picked up the phone again.

I called USC.

The secretary put me on hold for a long time before a man came on to the phone. He barely introduced himself, and I felt like an idiot.

When I told him what happened, and the letter I had in my hand, he said,

"You did what?"

I blurted out,

"I left my apartment full of furniture, I have my son with my family here and I also have my transcripts in my hand."

Dean Robert E. Tranquada said,

"I have to meet you".
"Come in tomorrow and let's talk."

I went in, taking the letter.

He opened it and dutifully reviewed the cover letter and each page of my transcripts.

I silently sat. I practically wanted to blend into the wall. In just a few magical moments, he said,

"You'll have to repeat all your core rotations, and I want you to take a month off to get situated."

"Then come to class and finish your second year."

"You're accepted."

I wanted to run and hug him, but I couldn't. I profusely thanked him and walked out the door, still not realizing how lucky I was. But I had faith in God. He got me into medical school, and He had to keep me in it.

After repeating my first year of medical school, I had to repeat my second year.

I repeated the first year of medical school and later repeated all my core rotations as a resident. This means that three times, I had to learn *everything twice: at ORU medical school, at USC medical school, and again as an anesthesiology resident at Stanford.*

While in my fourth year of medical school, after having "flashes of brilliance" in my Ob/Gyn final exam, I was asked to stay on to do Obstetrics and Gynecology Residency. But I did not want the life of a surgeon.

Instead, I chose the life of an anesthesiologist.

On my medical school Ob/Gyn rotation at USC, I decided to go into anesthesia. This came about through conversations with a Labor & Delivery Nurse Midwife, who talked me in to anesthesiology. She swore that I had to become an anesthesiologist. Her husband was an anesthesiologist and made good money, provided a good life.

In this third year of medical school, all my friends were interviewing all over the country for 20 different residency programs, spending a mini fortune traveling from city to city. We were all studying for National Board exams and waiting for the national "match" day when the programs picked their residents. They had easy elective rotations that allowed them to take time off. Everyone spent a mini fortune traveling from one residency training program to another.

Not me, cause I was still repeating my core rotations to graduate with my class. I believed God wanted me to go into anesthesiology, so I did the unthinkable—I only applied to one anesthesiology residency program.

I only applied to USC's anesthesia residency program.

And I got in.

A couple of years later, as a senior resident, I transferred to Stanford and completed anesthesiology residency there.

Stanford anesthesiology's conditional acceptance dictated that I repeat all my anesthesia core rotations already done at USC: Orthopedics, Hearts, Lungs, Ob/Gyn, and Pain Management. Everything had to be repeated.

This was the third time I had to repeat my training twice.

Upon graduating Stanford anesthesiology, I was accepted to the only Critical Care Fellowship Program I applied to: Stanford.

Then I applied to only one academic position after Fellowship, and I got it: Assistant Professor at the University of Pennsylvania.

For my medical school graduation present to myself, I bought a time share. Eventually, I traveled all over the world with it, from the Canadian Rockies to Hawaii, New York, Pennsylvania, the Caribbeans, Germany, Aruba, and more.

I loved Banff Lake and Lake Louise. I skied the most incredible mountains in Innesbrook and Garmesh.

I swam every pool I could find, even if it was snowing. My favorite part was walking along the heated walkway to jump in a frothing swimming pool because the water was so warm that it created its own hovering cloud over the pool.

It was a dream.

Five years later, when I was married and pregnant with my daughter, we went to South Korea, where I was received as an Honorary Professor of Seoul University's Department of Anesthesiology.

Pregnant women did not go out in public then, and I gained so much weight and looked *so* pregnant that mouths would drop. Literally. There were no chairs in restaurants; I got down on the floor to eat.

As the baby grew, we took her to various hotels in Chicago and Lake Arrowhead, where the swimming pool was halfway in the hotel and halfway outside the hotel. I took the baby and swam with her both indoors and outdoors, while it was snowing.

I'll never forget how tightly her little fists grabbed my arms. Here again, the water was so warm that it was steaming a good twelve feet above the water level.

The swim and the snow.

This was my kind of dreamland.

The Swim and The Snow. My kind of Dreamland.

No More Tears
Dr. Margaret Aranda

As an intern and resident at USC, I drove wherever I wanted and whenever I wanted. I gave drunks on the roadside sack lunches that I held outside my car for them to retrieve. I talked my way out of speeding tickets because I was on my way to donate blood, or I was late to work at the Jail Ward.

I knew that I was blessed to have used my body for so many decades, so much athleticism.

My swimming days seemed over. I knew the stark difference between being able and being disabled. And over time, I thought, "Maybe all those athletic years mademe more able to tolerate being disabled, more able to recover." Besides the physical dimension, mental health was an issue. At the end of this road to recovery, I didn't want to be bitter or resentful.

I forgave everyone for everything.

I concentrated on problems inside my head, and inside my body.

I wrote to save my brain.

While I was disabled, people asked me what advice I had for the well, the able.

Use your body now.

While you can, whether sick or well, use your body while you are able to move it.

Go ahead and revel in the swimming arm strokes, the running, the skiing, the team sports like racquetball and tennis.

Dance.

Go on missionary trips to third world countries and see how they live.

Help people help themselves.

Become the star in your own movie.

Make your life follow your dreams.

Travel.

But before you travel, I would ask one thing: read about the culture and language before you go.

In sharp contrast to my being able to move and be athletic virtually all my life, things were different now, and they were going to be different for a long time.

I was suddenly unable to move.

Being Disabled

Human dignity only happens as a moment-to-moment occurrence of action with your neighbor next door or the bagger at the grocery store. To know the name of the person who sweeps your office and empties your trash, to know how many kids they have, to give them a 'Happy Birthday" on their special day. Do you know the name of the person who empties your trash at work?

For tomorrow, you may not have a body that moves. And tomorrow, you may never be able to travel again.

But I can. The doctors are not always right. Miracles still happen, and God is still in your life. He gives life so that you may live more abundantly. Hold on to that promise.

People ask me,

"What was it like to be disabled?"

Some even comment, "Every doctor should be disabled to know what it feels like."

Well, I was never one of those doctors that people would wish would get ill. I don't think I "deserved" my life to go the way it did, but I know that no one deserves pain, suffering, loss of their spouse, child, and home.

Here is what it was like . . .

The Traumatic Brain Injury Ward

The hardest part was not being able to understand or to talk.

As an inpatient in the Brain Rehabilitation ward at Northridge Hospital, I sat around a big conference room table, with ten other patients and a lady giving a talk. I couldn't even say the word, "the" and had speech therapy every day for a month. Later, I would do five more courses of speech therapy.

Age 45: Wanting to Be a Bird

I remember looking up at her as she wrote on the chalkboard. Her hand was middle aged, younger than her face. She looked smart but she did not talk very smartly.

She was simple.

I was confused. I said to myself,

"That should be me up there."

I was not the guest lecturer on pulmonary hypertension, teaching a group of nursing students, nor the guest lecturer for The Management of Hypotension for the entire second year class at a major medical school.

I was not the guest lecturer at the international meeting about new technologies to assist in the management of ICU patients.

I was not the guest lecturer in Mainz, for the department of anesthesiology's residents at Johannes Gutenberg University where, instead of clapping, the Germans knocked their knuckles on their desks.

After lecture, we all went outside to a keg of beer, nicely displayed in the foyer. Astonishing. We can't drink beer during lecture or any other times in anesthesiology residency in the USA.

I was not in front of the Department of Anesthesiology in Seoul's Medical School, where I gave a lecture on "Ventilation/Perfusion (V/Q) Mismatch in the Intensive Care Unit." They bestowed upon me the title of "Honorary Professor," and it was a very humble and proud moment.

My mind struggled to remember,

"What am I doing here, again?"

I was used to being the one lecturer in a group of medical students, residents, nurses, fellows, and other students. After all, I knew about neurology, neuroanatomy, and neurosurgery and dissected a brain in medical school (honors to those who donated their body, their vessel).

What about my ER work at a military base? How could I ever again see one hundred patients per day and have the pleasure to serve those who serve my country?

My mind popped back into the room at the sound of the clickety-clack of the chalk on the chalk board.

I made my mind circle back to this lady with a piece of chalk in her hand.

She was actually telling us that when we leave the house, we must remember to . . . take our driver's license.

"Huh?"

"Remember to take your medications."

"What?" I was incredulous. Clearly, some mistake had been made and I wasn't supposed to be here!

She went on an on, and now her voice was deep . . . and deeper. Slower . . . And slower.

"Remember (garble - garble)".

I wanted to throw up.

I looked down.

Then I looked up.

"Who was I sitting with in this room, at this huge rectangular table?"

A man in his thirties sat on my right in a straight-backed wheelchair with a halo around his neck.

He was moaning and drooling, saliva dripping on a bib around his neck.

"WHAT THE HECK AM I DOING HERE? THERE HAS BEEN SOME KIND OF A MISTAKE! I DON'T BELONG HERE! I'M NOT LIKE . . . HIM!"

I wanted to run.

I wanted to fly.

I just wanted to BE a bird that could fly.

I didn't deserve to be cooped up here.

I looked around.

I knew what they all had, what they were: a patient with a traumatic brain injury.

I was one of them now.

I was in shock.

Again, I wanted to cry.

I wanted to run.

But I couldn't get up from my chair.

Days passed, then the month was almost over.

Only one person visited me, not my baby, not my ex-husband. Roxanne was a nurse anesthetist I used to work with at the VA, and she was sweet as honey. She probably drove two hours to see me.

During visiting hours, they brought me out to meet her. Of course, I recognized her. The nurse pulled my wheelchair next to her and left me there with her in the hallway. The window behind us was white and glowing, and she sat on a soft bench whose whiteness complemented the glow, as if they matched one another.

Roxanne looked at me. Plainly surprised and worried, she immediately started crying. I mean, she was bawling.

I didn't know why she was crying. I wanted to tell her not to cry for me.

But like a sad kitten, not one letter would come out.

I tried. Nothing would come out.

I could form the words in my brain.

I knew the word "hi" started with an "H." But my tongue, lips and throat could not and would not form into even the hint of a one-syllable word.

For almost a year, I could not say the word, "the."

After leaving the brain unit, it took an additional six courses of physical therapy to learn how to say the word, "the."

Being in a Wheelchair

It wasn't quite so bad to be in a wheelchair because that meant I was out of bed.

But because my body liked to lay down and not sit up, it took a while to get used to sitting in a wheelchair. For this reason, they wanted me to have a long-boarded wheelchair, not one that you can sit in. This would allow me to lay back a bit. But it was ugly, depressing. I couldn't do it.

It took three hours to dress and get ready, then sometimes it took another 30 minutes to even find a spot in the parking lot. Then the distance from the lot to a doctor's office appointment could be long and windy. By the time my appointment was over, and I had made it back to the car, I was exhausted and ready for a nap.

I had to keep drinking fluids and eating salt, to keep my blood pressure up. It was hard to stay around ice or various waters, to keep hydrated well beyond normal. Some days, I even salted my bananas to get more salt in my system.

The most depressing thing about being in a wheelchair was dressing up, making it out of the car, and then going to get something to eat. One restaurant we went to, a popular café on Santa Monica Boulevard, welcomed us into their dining area.

Upon looking in, everyone stopped eating and stared at me. There was no way the wheelchair could even get in between the tables and chairs to be seated anywhere in the establishment.

Time and time again, the wheelchair was cumbersome and unwanted.

I will compliment both the airlines and Disneyland for helping all of us in a wheelchair feel wanted and accommodated. It was a pleasure to fly.

Eventually, I started pushing my wheelchair instead of sitting in it.

Three and a half years had gone by.

Walking with a Walker

When I was strong enough to walk with a walker, it was liberating in many ways. No longer was I restrained from walking down narrow restaurant aisles, as I could ditch the walker at the door and carefully walk to my table.

I got tired easily though, and required a walker with a seat, because I frequently needed to sit down. It was still bulky, took up more length of space than a wheelchair, but folded flat.

I never fell in my walker, but I know others who have. I was still on a blood thinner, so avoiding falls was a big goal.

I was less ostracized in a walker, felt more freedom, and my IV bag could be cradled in the seat, so in many ways, it was liberating.

I also think it was less embarrassing to the public, who stared at me for shorter periods of time. And it was less embarrassing to me because I felt very unsure of myself in a wheelchair.

Compared to being in a wheelchair, walking with a walker was much better.

I used a walker for another three-and-a-half years.

I was now bedridden for seven years.

Walking with a Cane

It is not easy to walk with a cane, and the 'graduation' from walker to cane was much more trepid for me. I had to balance better and not use the cane for actual support.

I was gardening in the late afternoon one day and somehow almost tripped on my cane and fell on the cement. I may have cracked my head and sustained another head injury; still being on blood thinners, this near-fall tremendously scared me.

So, I threw my cane in the trash.

Another three-and-a-half years had passed.

Now, I was bedridden for twelve years.

Walking

Walking again made me feel 'normal.' I still had to be careful not to fall and was still on blood thinners.

I am very grateful that once out of a wheelchair, I never went back. Once out of the walker, I never went back. And that stupid cane was never going to be my friend. I never went back to a cane.

Being Able Again

Barring things like disease or a car accident; look at your general health. If you are healthy, that is wealth.

"Health" is a relative term. If you are not healthy, imagine you fell and broke an arm or leg, making everything worse. Or if you don't have arms or legs, imagine you had a heart attack or a stroke, making everything worse. If you have chronic back pain and eat ice cream all the time, you will gain weight and your back pain will get worse.

If you have any medical problem whatsoever and you eat ice cream all the time, you will become diabetic. If you become diabetic, you may lose your eyesight, kidney, and maybe one or both legs. If you are lucky, you may get a kidney transplantation. But you must realize that would leave you on significant steroids for the rest of your life. You will gain weight, develop a hump of fat on the back of your neck, and get "truncal obesity" where you forever lose a waistline. You can have a silent heart attack, a diabetic storm with sugars out of control, a leg infection, become septic with a blood infection in your arteries, and die on a ventilator in the ICU because you're on those steroids. So, stop eating so much ice cream.

We are talking about keeping what you have.

There are certain things no one can ever take away from you.

Some are out of your control a bit, like your wealth, which may depend on your abilities, other people, or the environment. Your diet and the food you eat are primarily in your control because you are the one that orders food and gets groceries. Or you tell other people what you want.

Since the food you eat controls main components of your health and longevity, we can say with confidence that you must eat every day. Know that whatever you put in your mouth either hurts or helps you.

The beautiful thing is that God built our bodies to get *better* the more they are used. Unlike an automobile with planned obsolescence, he did not program us to get old and die; he created us in his image, to live forever.

You can master this and be the best you can be.

Your next step is to make this decision: to keep your body on track and out of my office.

Here are the two ways we can eat:

1. With premium gas for maximal performance and longevity.
2. With cheap gas and for average performance, early demise, and more doctor visits.

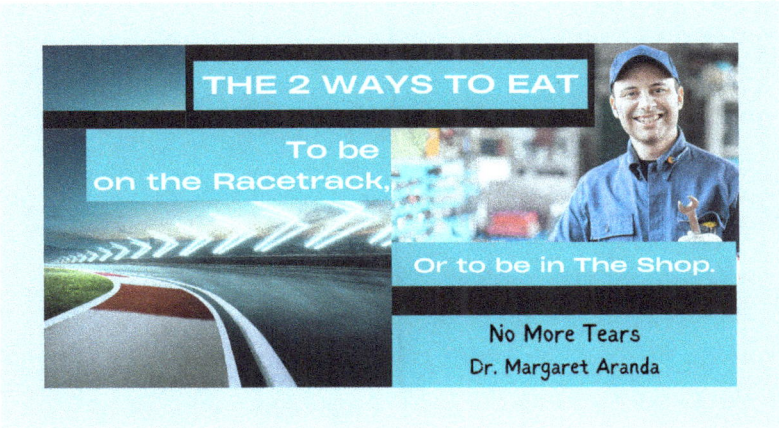

Everything I put into my body matters for quality of life and longevity.

We will remain optimistic and say that no matter what your health is, sickness is like having your body in the shop all the time. Honestly, as a physician, I don't need to have you keep coming in often to see me because you are sick. I would much rather have you either not come in at all because you are well, or come in to stay well.

Maintenance is a priority: being in shape, having strength, being trim, eating the right foods, taking supplements, as well as preventing COVID and initiating early treatment for any disease.

Wellness is like having your body on the racetrack. You are the one that defines your wellness, so do the best you can to put food in your house that helps you live longer.

"Health is wealth."

No one can take the health you have away from you.

If we have the attitude that we control our own body, *we control our future.*

I know this because I am never going to be that sick again. I could have done things differently—I could have learned what I know from someone else who suffered ahead of me and told me what to do and what not to do. I hope this book works for you in this way.

The more disabled you are, the better you show an improvement and the more you can "awe" those around you! Doesn't that excite you?

When I got out of my wheelchair and stood up in a walker, no one recognized me. Similarly, when I started walking and wearing dresses and high heels again, no one recognized me. I could literally be in a store with people that *knew me,* and they would not know that it was me. It was like I was invisible.

The more improved you are over time, even if it is 1% a month, that adds up to 12% in a year and almost *25% better in two years!* Just think of how *good* you'll look, how awesome you'll feel, and the things you'll be able to *do* when you're better.

See yourself getting better than anyone expected you to be. See yourself looking younger as the years go by, when everyone else around you ages.

See yourself getting stronger when others are losing strength. Then *do something*. Lift cans of tomato sauce, walk, or ride a stationary bike. Go to the park and sit on the grass. Eat an apple or a chunk of real cheese. Chew on frozen grapes or blueberries.

Time is going by anyway.

Do something with it.

Maybe by next Christmas, you will surprise yourself. Or perhaps by next 4th of July or Hannukah, you'll surprise your family.

Do something today, now.

Put this book down. Get up and start walking or rolling; go outside and sit in the sun. Take a book with you.

Then Tweet me @TheRebelPatient and let me know how you did!

Losing My Best Friends

The day after the accident, Anne said she thought there was something very wrong with me and that I shouldn't be sleeping so much. Very lovingly, she had me call her before I fell asleep and then again when I awoke.

We spoke like this several times a day. She even offered to come over day or night should I take a turn for the worse. She was a professional dog trainer in a very ritzy part of town, and I knew how busy she was, so her efforts were not lost on me.

She also loved my dog, Chuck, and worried about my being able to care for him. Chuck was a huge black lab that eventually grew to the size of a Great Dane. He was playful, strong, and smart but no one knew how big and gigantic he was going to be.

Anne was my best friend. She talked me into going to see my primary care provider (PCP).

She saved my life.

In the first days, I took her advice, drove myself a jaunt away to a doctor's appointment, was wiped out on arrival, and spent the entire doctor's exam time curled up in a fetal position.

The doctor talked to my back instead of talking to me. He did not even look at my face. I could have been someone else. So, when I wriggled my neck an inch to turn to try to see him, I could only hold it up for a small time while before it collapsed.

With fervor, he seemed to spend a lot of time writing things down and filling out forms. My back was to him the entire time. He never looked me in the eye, or even in the face. I was a bunch of numbers held together by their master, time.

And time was not on my side.

Anne was mortified.

I do not recall receiving a physical examination to assess my neurological status, but I do recall being given some free samples of skin lotion for my sun poisoning.

Later, I got what I needed, a Medrol dose pack of methylprednisolone to decrease the inflammation. My lips were puffed out as if they just got a collagen implant, and my sick LA girlfriends (not Anne) were jealous of my oversized lips!

I was in pain and my voice was sore. As an anesthesiologist, I knew that my airway was swollen the same way as if I had been bitten by a bee; this was an anaphylactic emergency, and the steroids were helping.

After a traumatic brain injury, it is an area of controversy about whether to give steroids right away. I wanted them for my sun poisoning, but they had to have lowered my brain inflammation.

Weeks later, Anne drove to see me in our new home, and I knew the drive was an hour in LA traffic. Again, my senses were heightened because I knew it must be important, so her presence accentuated my concerns for my own condition.

No one else cared. Only Anne.

The second time she visited me, Chuck had almost pushed me into the now drained swimming pool we were redesigning. I would have fallen into the deep end, which was 11-foot-deep. I would have died. Or I would have been home alone with Madi, who was still only age 2.

We decided Chuck was too big a risk for me. We regretfully ended up giving him away to a great home with a huge back yard. I think Anne was always sad that she didn't take him for herself . . . he was a great dog.

I don't have Anne in my life anymore, not Anne or any high school, college, or medical school friends.

No one.

I guess no one wanted to know a brain-injured person. Maybe they were uncomfortable around me, or they didn't know what to say.

Maybe I embarrassed them. They certainly couldn't embarrass me, because I did not possess the kind of capacity that could experience embarrassment.

What do you say to a brain-injured person?

"I'm praying for you. I know you will get better. I speak life into your life. I pray God springs forth new beginnings each morning you awaken. I pray the Holy Spirit leads you and guides you in all the ways you should go. I know that God will open the doors that need to be opened and close all the doors that need to be closed."

Talk to any sick person at home or in the hospital as if they are normal. Speak to them, say their name, trigger their brain.

But there was no one there to pray for me, to read to me, or to sing to me.

Maybe they figured I would never notice.

. . . because they thought I was going to die.

~ ~ ~ ~ ~ ~ ~ ~ ~ ~

Age 5: The Edge of the Pool

I crawled out of the pool, breathless. I ate a pink cupcake then quietly, I put on her red and white peppermint sandals to go to the pool.

It was a big party outside, many people swimming about. All the kids and grown-ups were there. Lots of bright colors to match the bright day, pink balloons, brown leaves on the edge of the pool, first calm then screaming, running, bustle of a party. Kids jumping in, Whoosh! Splashes!

I knew how to swim, I did. Every Mommy was laying in the sun, on a green chair that was crisscrossed, weaved in and out. It was not built too well, because I saw all Mommy's bodies went through the holes like lumps in the chair. Sunken in, pooches sticking out here and there. It was not a good chair at all. Anyway, I knew I wasn't supposed to stare.

I had just been in the pool too long. I wanted to get out.

I was tired, the kids were too loud, the sun was too hot, and I just had enough. I was a big girl now, five years old.

So, I decided to do it.

I saw the wall, the Edge of the Pool.

The lady on the floatie thing wouldn't even know I was swimming under her.

I took a huge breath. I was going to swim under the lady, bright blue water swaying to and fro. It was not too far away.

One big breath, Whoosh! Whooooooooo! Huuuupppppp! Go!

My lungs were filled.

First all hands, then my whole body went under the water. I kicked and kicked.

For five years old, it was not too far away, that Edge of the Pool. Maybe five more kicks.

I was under the water, swimming under the lady with the poochy chair. She was still floating on that big balloon and wouldn't even notice me.

At first, it was just a feeling that I was running out of breath.

I thought I could do it.

It was not far. But then something started to change . . .

I was definitely running out of breath. I must go up for air!

I went up!

Something went BUMP!

It was blurry, light blue, like the color of the water. It was big. It was floating.

I could not push my head up to get to any air.

I could not stand up.

I could not push the lady on the floatie thing away. I was stuck.

There was no more air.

My lungs were going to burst, my eyes were popping out.

I was stuck under that big blue thing floating. Something was up there. It was in my way! I tried to push it! It won't budge and that lady doesn't even know I'm under her!

No one knows I'm here!

Somewhere up there, I could hear the clinking of wine glasses and the chuckles of a lady who was sitting on the floating blue thing eating the same pink cupcake like I ate.

Sounds were far away now.

Fading, going gray.

My heartbeat was beating in my ears.

Bump, bump . . . bump, bump.

In a flash, I knew the lady would never hear her, would never see her, would never feel anything. Each of my lungs was about to burst.

I was alone.

I decided that my only chance was to

Go.
Back.
Down.

I could not struggle under the big blue thing floating.

I smashed my eyes closed and teeth gritted.

Kicked a last few kicks and went down, down, down, kicking, kicking, kicking.

Floating under the big blue thing with the lady and the clanging and the chuckles. I went under it and now I was not sure which way I should go.

Was it left? Or right?
Uk. Oh.

Things were going darker gray. I went straight, because I thought that was where the edge of the pool was.

I kicked and I kicked, and I kicked and stretched all hands out, my little hands wAaAay out, the hands that loved to play with my kittens.

I stretched my little hands out as far, far, as far as they could go far far . . . BUMP!

The wall! The edge of the pool!

My fingers reached it. Nice!

I crept all my fingers up the edge of that pool, and in slow motion, my head, then my ears, then my nose surfaced over the water and into the air and

I INHALED!!!!

I INHALED A raspy, DEEP, big, huge, GINORMOUS breath.

I was gasping, sobbing.

My shoulders leaned up on the edge of the pool.

Dangling legs, weak and prickly. Could hardly move.

I looked around, wiping tears one-handed.

Bloodshot eyes.

No one noticed.

Everyone thought ie was just water in my eyes.

I never told anyone. I thought I would get in trouble.

When my mom reads this, she is going to cry because that day at the pool party, I almost died. And no one would have known until my body was limp and lifeless, filled with water.

I only tell you now because I know I can't get in trouble anymore. But never again did I ever swim under a floaty thing. Never. And when I grew up and had babies of my own, I never, ever let them put floaties in the pool.

Not once.

Never.

I crawled out of the pool, breathless.

I realized what happened.

I almost died.

And no one.

Even.

Noticed.

~ ~ ~ ~ ~ ~ ~ ~ ~ ~

That was then and this was now.

Life repeated itself.

My Full-Time Job

Initially, I was bedridden for months that stretched into more than one year. I spent every day throwing up, being sickly and stuck in my bed. I was unaware of all my surroundings.

I woke up and threw up. Everything made me throw up: breakfast, being a car passenger, moving too fast, bending, sitting, moving. Everything. I was unable to go down a grocery store aisle; if I did, I could not scan my eyes to get a view of things on a shelf. Scanning my eyes made me throw up.

If I did scan an aisle, I needed to stop, put my hand over my mouth, and try not to throw up. I could only tolerate being in a store for five to ten minutes before I was ataxic, nauseated, pale, and gaunt. It sapped the life out of me.

Zofran didn't work well, Phenergan didn't either, but I took one or the other around the clock for a decade. If I was nauseated and needed to be awake, it was Zofran under the tongue. If I was overtired and nauseated and needed to be asleep, it was Phenergan as a rectal suppository. Because of the medications that stopped me from throwing up, I was able to keep my weight—or else I would have been a skeleton.

To try to decrease visual stimulation, I wore a hat with 'blinders' on the sides, pulled over to cut out my peripheral vision. Like racehorses who can only see in front of them, I could only focus on what was in front of my eyes. If I had too much in my visual field, I would throw up in the store.

I also had to wear dark sunglasses even at nighttime, because my eyes were not used to the light. They were slightly and permanently dilated, and no one could tell me why. Light went to the back of my brain, piercing it to the core and rendering me helpless. Like a Prisoner of War for a decade, the sun was my enemy. Eventually, the sun gave me hives and I had to wear sunproof clothing, covering every inch of my skin.

Then, we noted antihistamines helped. After about eight years, we learned I had Mast Cell Activation Syndrome (MCAS). This was relieved by an antihistamine diet, and it slowly faded.

Since a rare occurrence with MCAS is mast cell sarcoma, which as a terrible mortality, I had to undergo a bone marrow to check for cancerous mast cells. This was a very painful procedure done under general anesthesia, and I was grateful that during the "opioid crisis", my hematologist/oncologist gave me a few days of opioids.

After breakfast, I laid in bed with my legs to the ceiling. Then I put on thigh-high Jobst stockings that squeezed the blood out of my legs, pushing it upward and into my belly. This way, when I stood up, the blood was redistributed so that my brain got more blood.

Wearing stockings was difficult on hot days when it caused sweating and the attending loss of salt and water. And it was uncomfortable, but I did it. I felt like an old lady wearing thick tan stockings that were not sexy at all . . . but I did it because it allowed me to stand up without fainting. I also had to take medication to help that issue, but this was a great physical thing that corrected an underlying deficit, that of dysautonomia.

To see doctors and to get better, I had to function.

Gradually, I had not just one doctor, but five: primary care, allergist, neurologist, neurosurgeon, and a cardiologist. I also had physical therapy, speech therapy, and occupational therapy. I had to pick up medications from several pharmacies because nothing came in the mail, and nothing was timed so it all was ready once a month; for years, it seemed that everything came in at different times until someone corrected it.

I longed for Mondays and Fridays, glorious days when we avoided having a doctor's appointment.

After weeks of physical therapy, occupational therapy, speech therapy, and multiple doctor visits, I was more interested in what was left in my brain, not what I lost in my brain.

I wanted to remember things. I played Scrabble for the mental stimulation, avoiding frustration at the actual score. My Uncle David gifted me a Scrabble game when he visited our home. In the beginning, I could not look at the game board when it had to be moved for the next player's view; it made me nauseated.

Just when I thought things couldn't be worse, I tore my right shoulder, the supraspinatus tendon at the rotator cuff. I still had a PICC line in the left arm.

After taking so long to get better, people started to say I looked beautiful. I saw myself without the IV. The doctors said that would never happen. But I looked at the sky and the stars. I saw myself persevering through all these obstacles. I knew God was watching over me, and I trusted being in his care.

My job was to get better, and I could not rely on just the doctors to get me better—my health was in God's hands, not theirs.

I had to participate in the healing process. For a time, I couldn't move, so I had to just lay around.

But if I *could move*, I should. I needed to get my life back.

I told myself:

"Wake up. Get up. Get out of bed."

"You have to do it, or you will die."

"You must do it. "

Being an Anesthesiologist

Age 35: Walking Down the Hallway

People cared about what I said. Their eyes waited for me to speak.

At Stanford, I was finally treated like I was smart, like my thoughts and questions had value. It deeply affected my self-confidence, so I flourished.

Whereas I was literally up all night at USC doing trauma cases all night, now I slept through the nights. There was so little trauma that I checked my beeper to see if it was working.

I called the hospital operator.

"Can you please page me?"

She laughed, "Sure, doctor. I'll page you right now."

By the time a few On Call Nights passed, the hospital operators knew I would call them to check my beeper. Eventually, I learned to sleep through the night.

During the day, Stanford anesthesiology was nothing like USC. At USC, I was in the operating room all day and into the evening, sometimes not getting lunch relief or barely getting a sack lunch because there was no time to go down to the Doctor's Dining Room.

At Stanford, I did not spend all day in the operating room. We got a morning break and went into the Breakfast Room, drinking coffee and eating muffins with the attendings we admired so much.

It was here that I met wonderful anesthesiologists like Myer Rosenthal, MD, Ronald G. Pearl, MD, PhD, Tom Feeley, MD, and Fred Mihm, MD. They were to be my ICU Attendings as a Fellow. They mingled with us, made us feel at home, and valued our thoughts and opinions.

I also met the Pain Management Anesthesiologists like Ray Gaeta, MD, and others who attended an inpatient ward dedicated to taking patients off opioids in a gradual and blinded fashion. They received medications as a liquid and signed a contract that they would not know how much drug it contained.

Each morning, I learned how to decrease dosing, what the effects were, and how to tell if someone was lying.

Upon admission into the program, my Attending would hand me a 20 ml gigantic syringe of fentanyl. Then they would say,

"See how much he needs."

I'm thinking,

"I've never done this before."

But my Attending made it sound so easy,

"Just titrate it in until the pupils get small and keep asking him how he feels. Get a pain score every 10 minutes or so. Be sure you know where the pain is, and the description."

And with that, POOF! The Attending was gone, and I would be left alone in the room to give a patient on high-dose opioids continuous boluses of fentanyl, 50 mcg at a time.

I would put in the IV then start dosing. In the beginning, the pupils were large, as the patient was behind on medication dosing. Some were already starting to withdraw, so they would be sweaty, and the blood pressure and heart rates would both be very high.

Over time, I learned how to look at the pupils, ask the patient how much pain they were in, and then determine if their last medication dose should still be working.

As I sat with a patient over about an hour, invariably their pupils would become tiny, very pinpoint. I mean itsy, bitsy, tiny.

If I then asked how much pain they had, I knew by looking at the eyes that they could feel the medication. If they said,

"Oh, I don't feel a thing. I still have pain that is a 10/10", I knew they were lying.

No one really lied, though. Everyone wanted to go off opioids and that is why they were here. No one went through withdrawal as they were slowly eased down on dosing. Some stayed a month, others stayed shorter or longer.

It was a very gradual process, but very rewarding for both the patient and the physicians.

One patient was so grateful that she had a dozen plump, faint peach-colored roses delivered to the room and then surprised me with them.

I received more roses from patients than from men.

At Stanford, I learned what my father had taught me my whole life long:

*"Margaret, I can't **believe** I get paid for what I do all day! I would do it for free! I love going to work in the mornings! I love my job!"*

At Stanford, I felt the same way. I missed it when I was gone.

I absolutely loved going to work every day. The nurses treated me with respect, my team was solid, my attendings were amazing, and they lectured several times a week.

Attendings relieved us in the operating room and let us go to planned lectures that made the program most cohesive.

By the time I finished Stanford's anesthesiology residency, I had the best of both worlds: high clinicals and low academics at USC, and less tiring clinicals and high academics at Stanford.

In different ways, I was grateful for both programs, which complimented one another.

Clinical and academic, I had the best of both worlds.

The IV drops were for me now, instead of my patients.

For a decade, I watched those tear-shaped drops fall into my IV line.

I knew how to change IV bags. Was it God's sense of humor that as an anesthesiologist and a patient, my road in life leads me to being surrounded by bags of IV fluids?

I told myself that I was going on with my life *in Christ*. I had to persevere.

I had to fight.

I didn't want to take 'no' for an answer. I believed that God was guiding my steps.

When I applied to medical school, I didn't know if I would get accepted. But I knew that if God wanted me to be a doctor, he would get me in. Again, when I applied to internship, residency and then to Fellowship, I didn't know if I would get in. But I only applied to two internships, one residency and one Fellowship, because I wanted God to show himself to me.

My attitude? I had a one in a million chance of getting into medical school or residency. If God did that for me, then if I had a one in a million chance of recovering, God would also do that for me.

My *choices* made me who I was.

I chose to watch those drops fall and I felt them bring life.

So, on the one hand, I loved that IV. I depended upon and cherished my PICC line, even though it kept getting infected and clotted.

And on the other hand, when it got infected or clotted, I hated that IV line. I hated the drops, the tear-shaped *drip, drops*, and the *hum, drum* of the battery pack. They followed me everywhere and were a thorn in my side.

Anesthesiologists make quick decisions. We run codes, we transfuse blood, we ask for help, we call Codes. We intubate, hydrate, add pressor therapy, and wrack our brains to keep people alive, with only seconds to spare until permanent brain injury occurs.

Age 40: Being in A Far Corner

I was an Attending now, both in the Surgery/Traumatology ICU and the Outpatient Clinic at the University of Pennsylvania, quite a way from the Main Operating Rooms (ORs). My assigned patient was here for a routine dental procedure, not an emergency.

He was large, had a very big neck, and I knew he would be a difficult intubation. I had to put a breathing tube in, connect it to the ventilator, and mechanically breathe for him, to facilitate his dental procedure.

Each morning, I arrived the Outpatient Clinic ahead of time, and checked my suction, oxygen, airway, anesthesia machine, medications, IV fluids and tubing. I ran the ventilator and made sure it worked, breathing oxygen into a bag.

Unbeknownst to me, all my experience and preparation was going to be put to the test.

As I prepared to put his breathing tube in, perhaps he had an acute asthma attack at the same time.

Suddenly, my patient was turning blue.

I could not see his vocal cords, where my tube needed to be. He was not going to be able to breathe.

Even though he was breathing on his own, he was not getting enough oxygen. His belly bopped upwards, distending, and plopping his lungs shut at the bases.

We had 3 minutes to save his brain.

I called a CODE.

It was the only time I ever did that in my life, but I did it.

I asked for help.

Another anesthesiologist came into the room and helped me on the airway. He held the patient's head and jaw while I pumped the bag to get molecules of air into the patient's lungs.

We waited for help to arrive and were able to get his oxygenation better. But he was gray now, not blue. Gray was a better color than blue, but it still was not a good color.

He was in bronchospasm now, and his vocal cords were closing. I could feel that the bag was getting harder to squeeze with both of my little hands.

I called for an ENT surgeon STAT!

"I need a trach!"

"Are you sure?" the Circulating Nurse asked, and if my eyes didn't speak for my masked face, I said it again,

"NOW! CALL!"

She grabbed the overhead intercom to the entire hospital, paging ENT to come to OR 7, STAT!

Within literally 30 seconds, a team arrived with a tray of instruments, and in no time, secured an airway. They were seamless, artful, professional and confident, instilling that confidence in all of us.

Had I waited another 30 seconds to call a Code, he would have died literally in my hands.

We later learned that the patient was the brother of one of our prominent cardiology staff, and while no one would be happy waking up from dental surgery with a hole in their neck from the tracheostomy, he was indeed very happy and grateful to be alive.

He didn't remember a thing.

Now I lived like an anesthesiologist in that I used every morsel of knowledge that I had in me to constantly, 24/7 make the best decisions for my survival.

I got out of my bed when no one thought I could walk.

When nobody thought I'd get out of a wheelchair, I started walking with my walker.

Then they thought I'd need a walker for life. I worked to prove them wrong.

There was a day that I did jumping jacks in my cardiologist's office. He didn't look at me like I was crazy.

He knew that I was a miracle.

Being a Woman Anesthesiologist

In the first few weeks of my traumatic brain injury, I complained that the doctors weren't taking me seriously. I needed backup.

My husband cleared his calendar so that from this point forward, he would go with me to doctor appointments. I thought this would make my care better, and that he would command respect.

It was obvious that all the male doctors now spent more time looking at and talking to him, instead of me.

In fact, one of them literally ignored me while talking to my ex-husband, and I was starting to wretch. My heaves got bigger and bigger until they finally noticed just in time to hand me a trash can.

I promptly vomited.

From then on, I paid more attention to who wasn't paying attention to me.

If I was talking and I could see they weren't even really listening, I would literally stop talking in the middle of my sentence.

My neurologist, gratefully, erred on the side of using caution rather than tossing me aside as just another histrionic, depressed female with post-traumatic stress disorder (PTSD). He used common sense, intelligence, and kept me free from further harm.

Over the course of time and multiple specialty evaluations, my neurosurgeon knew of and referred me to a cardiologist who 'mayknow something.'

It was the best referral I ever had, because it turned out that my cardiologist knew everything.

For this reason, if you know something is wrong with you and you cannot get a diagnosis, I implore you to ditch one doctor after another until you find someone who knows something about your complaints.

My cardiologist sent me for the standard of care, a tilt table test. The tilt test provided my then final diagnosis—dysautonomia. Which means that when I stood up, I fainted.

No one ever heard of dysautonomia before, and it was new to all of us.

My piece of advice on doctor visits is not to go to see the doctor by yourself, especially if you are female. I believe that the level of male comradery is high, and too bad but us females, even if we are doctors ourselves, are still females.

It helped that I was a doctor, but it didn't help that much.

I was repeatedly dismissed as a histrionic female.

I was yelled at, treated disrespectfully, incredulously told on the one hand to "just be your own doctor," and then on the other hand,

"You need to be the patient, not the doctor."

Age 48: Being Treated Like A Woman

There were two instances I must share with you. Both occurred when I was by myself with a male doctor, both in the hospital as a patient.

The first doctor was sent in to try to figure out why I fainted when I stood up. At the end of our conversation, he said, "Do you just want me to prescribe Valium? I can give you some Valium."

I said, "No. If you don't know what's wrong with me, why don't you just tell me?"

I learned for myself how dangerous it can be for doctors to not just say, "I don't know."

Because if they would just take my word for it and believe my symptoms and history, I don't care that they don't know what my diagnosis is. But send me to someone who may know. Just say,

> "I don't know what is wrong with you, but let's try to find you someone who may be able to figure it out. They can at least provide another perspective."

It's not that much to ask. Don't insult me by offering me Valium.

At least that doctor did not harm me.

The second doctor did.

I had been better. I was well enough to walk, and I started remembering many different things.

I was very kindly accepted to go back to Stanford and do another year of clinicals, to get back my ability to work in an operating room again.

But I woke up one morning ataxic again. I could not walk in a straight line. I went to my cardiologist, who admitted me to the hospital.

In the hospital, he requested a neurology consultation. The neurologist came into my room and asked me to stand up. I stood. Then he asked me to close my eyes.

I could stand, but I told him that I could not close my eyes without falling. He assured me that if I fell, he would catch me.

So, I waited for him to tell me when, and then I closed my eyes. That's the last thing I remembered before opening them again.

I was on the floor looking at his shoes. They had not moved an inch.

I WAS ON THE FLOOR LOOKING AT HIS FLAWLESS SHOES

THEY HAD NOT MOVED AN INCH

No More Tears
Dr. Margaret Aranda

By the time I was hoisted up, I could see his disgust depicted by his hand on his hip, head pointing to the sky. I was furious.

I called my nurse, my charge nurse. I told her to write what happened in her notes. Soon thereafter, the hospital Patient Relations office, the CEO, and the Department of Neurology would each get a letter from me.

No one ever wrote or even called me back.

After that fall, I had suffered my second traumatic brain injury (TBI) and my second bout of diabetes insipidus (DI).

My pituitary gland banged on the wall of my brain's ventricle again, and I lost the ability to hold on to water.

I had to give up the Stanford position.

I lost my career (or so I thought).

More importantly, I lost my brain again and had a horrific complication, requiring a need for DDAVP injections to make my body hold on to water.

I contacted two attorneys about filing a malpractice claim. Because I was in the room alone with him, and there was no witness, they both advised me not to sue.

I lived with this medication for another year, and eventually I weaned myself off it, thank goodness. It is a horribly concentrated medication that was unforgiving.

On one hospitalization, the nurse injected me with too high a dose that caused my body to hold on to an enormous amount of water.

My head swelled and my eyes bulged out; they felt like they were going to pop out of my head.

I was a balloon full of water and my brain pounded with sharpness.

They had to stop the IV and just let the overdose fade away by itself, which took several more days.

It was to my advantage that I was a doctor, but to my disadvantage that I was a woman doctor.

In this case, it hurt me.

I didn't like being a victim of that circumstance.

I resolved to just get better again.

So, I started over again, from a wheelchair.

Recovering from Physical Disability

There are different reasons for being bedbound or wheelchair bound. I am sharing specifics on how I recovered and what worked for me.

Increase Mobility

If you are immobilized, talk to your doctor or physical therapist.

Exercise whatever part(s) of your body that you are able. If you can get into pool therapy, get into a swimming pool. It will not only lift your heart, but it sends an array of sensory input from your arms, legs, and torso to your brain.

Your brain can then 'relearn' the location of your own silhouette.

Ask your doctor if you could benefit from having a reclining bicycle at home. There is a type that sits on the floor, at low elevation. Getting your heart and major muscles pumping helps a lot of things, including your ability to catch yourself if you fall.

Increase Muscle Mass

Do not let your body go to waste; work to make your working parts excel. Strengthen your muscles whenever possible, and start off by taking measurements of your biceps, etc. Then every month, re-take measurements to see areas of improvement.

Keep on pushing gently to increase your strength, balance, and dexterity.

Decrease Total Body Fat

If you are overweight, it is much harder to pick yourself up. To decrease total body fat, talk to your doctor about intermittent fasting, a low glycemic diet, and a metabolic detox program.

People always ask me which diet program I prefer, and I like the Metagenics® products listed in the Appendix. In today's climate, I like patients to start with a liver and metabolic detoxification, using either Metagenics® or The Root Brands® products (See Appendix).

The less fat you have, the longer you will live, since heart problems are the number one cause of death.

Attaining a normal body weight maximizes your chances of success with achieving both a stronger body and mind.

Prayers that SPEAK LIFE

I could not have recuperated without prayer. Prayers came from me, and prayers came from my family and friends. Of all the friends that helped me, they were on social media: Jeffrey, MaryAnn, Bob across the pond, and more.

I read many healing verses from Scripture that were powerful to be spoken into my home and the very air around me.

Jeremiah 30:17
>   I will restore health to you, and your wounds I
>   will heal, declares the Lord.

Jeremiah 33:6

Nevertheless, I will bring health and healing to it; I will heal my people and will let them enjoy abundant peace and security.

Micah 7:8

When I fall, I will arise; when I sit in darkness, the Lord will be a light to me.

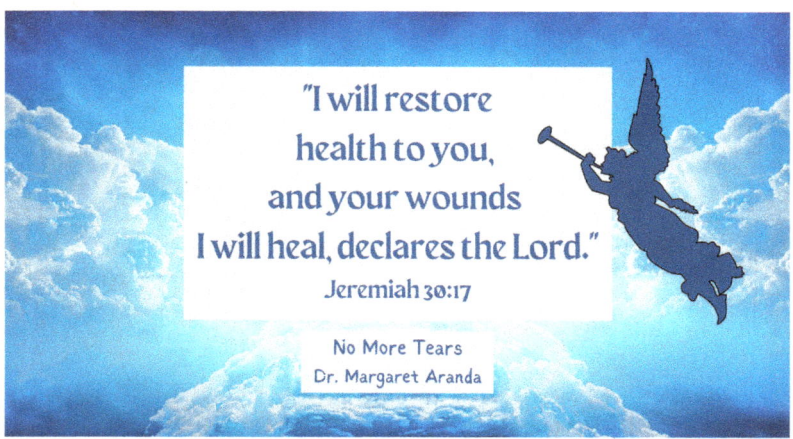

"I will restore health to you, and your wounds I will heal, declares the Lord."
Jeremiah 30:17

No More Tears
Dr. Margaret Aranda

Malachi 4:2

But for you who fear My name, the sun of righteousness shall rise with healing in its wings. You shall go out leaping like calves from the stall.

Psalms 30:2

O Lord, my God, I cried to you, and you have healed me.

Psalms 46:1

God is our refuge and strength, an ever-present help in trouble.

Psalms 46:5

God is within her, she will not fail.

Psalms 103:2-5

Praise the Lord, my soul, and forget not all his benefits. Who forgives all your sins and heals all your diseases, who redeems your life from the pit and crowns you with love and compassion, who satisfies your desires with good things so that your youth is renewed like the eagle's.

Psalms 147:3

He heals the brokenhearted and binds up their wounds.

Proverbs 4:20-22

My child, pay attention to what I say. Listen carefully to my words. Don't lose sight of them. Let them penetrate deep into your heart, for they bring life to those who find them, and healing to their whole body.

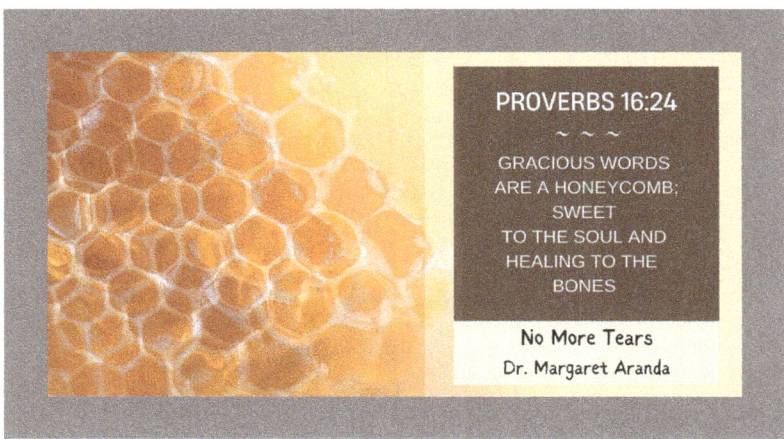

PROVERBS 16:24

~ ~ ~

GRACIOUS WORDS
ARE A HONEYCOMB;
SWEET
TO THE SOUL AND
HEALING TO THE
BONES

No More Tears
Dr. Margaret Aranda

Isaiah 41:10

Fear not, for I am with you; be not dismayed, for I am your God. I will strengthen you, yes, I will help you, I will uphold you with my righteous right hand.

Isaiah 53:5

But he was wounded for our transgressions, he was bruised for our iniquities: the chastisement of our peace was upon him; and with his stripes we are healed.

Isaiah 58:8

Your light will break forth like the dawn, and your healing will quickly appear.

Jeremiah 17:14

Heal me, O Lord, and I shall be healed; save me, and I shall be saved, for you are my praise.

Exodus 15:26

I am the Lord who heals you.

Exodus 23:25

I will take away all sickness from you.

2 Kings 20:5

I have heard your prayer and seen your tears. I will heal you.

Mark 5:29

She touched his cloak, and her bleeding stopped at once; and she had the feeling inside herself that she was healed of her trouble.

Mark 5:34

Your faith has healed you. Go in peace and be freed from your suffering.

3 John 1:2

Dear friend, I hope all is well with you and that you are as healthy in body as you are strong in spirit.

Matthew 9:22

Jesus turned, and seeing her he said, "Take heart daughter, your faith has made you well." And instantly the woman was made well.

Matthew 9:28-30

Then he touched their eyes (of the blind men) and said, "According to your faith let it be done to you." And their eyes were opened.

Matthew 11:28

> Then Jesus said, "Come to me, all of you who are weary and carry heavy burdens, and I will give you rest."

Matthew 28:20

> I am with you always.

Luke 8:50

> When Jesus heard this, he responded, "Don't be afraid; just keep trusting, and she will be healed."

Acts 10:38

> How God anointed Jesus of Nazareth with the Holy Spirit and with power, who went about doing good and healing all who were oppressed by the devil, for God was with him.

Romans 8:18

> Yet what we suffer now is nothing compared to the glory he will reveal to us later.

Romans 8:28

> And we know that all things work together for good to those who love God, to those who are called according to his purpose.

Romans 10:17

> So, then faith cometh by hearing, and hearing by the word of God.

1 Corinthians 13:7

> So, whether you eat or drink or whatever you do, do it all for the glory of God.

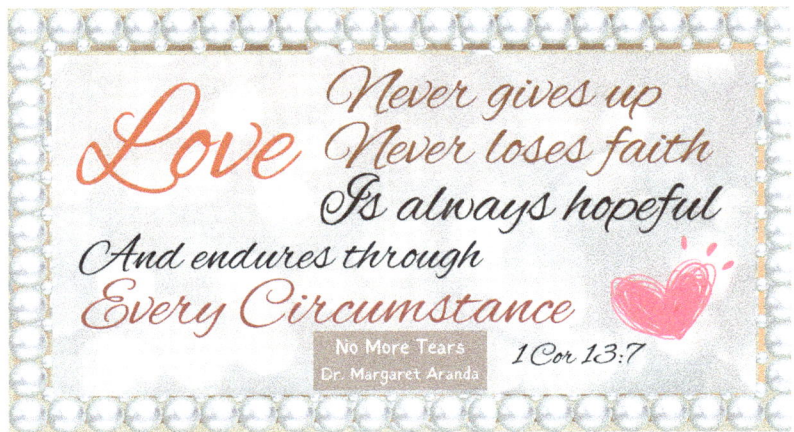

2 Corinthians 12:9-10

But he said to me, "My grace is sufficient for you, for my power is made perfect in weakness.

Therefore, I will boast all the more gladly of my weaknesses, so that the power of Christ may rest upon me. For the sake of Christ, then, I am content with weaknesses, insults, hardships, persecutions, and calamities. For when I am weak, then I am strong.

Philippians 3:12

I press on because Christ Jesus has made me his own.

For God has not
given us
a spirit of fear,
but of power & love,
and of a sound mind.

2 Timothy 1:7

No More Tears
Dr. Margaret Aranda

James 5:14

Is any one of you sick? He should call the elders of the church to pray over him and anoint him with oil in the name of the Lord.

James 5:15-16

And the prayer of faith will save the one who is sick, and the Lord will raise him up. And if he has committed sins, he will be forgiven.

Confess your faults to one another, and pray for one another, that ye may be healed. The effectual fervent prayer of a righteous man availeth much.

Hebrews 12:12-13

Lift up your tired hands, then, and strengthen your trembling knees! Keep walking on straight paths, so that the lame foot may not be disabled, but instead be healed.

Revelations 21:4

He will wipe away every tear from their eyes. Death will be no more. There will be no mourning, crying, or pain anymore, for the former things have passed away.

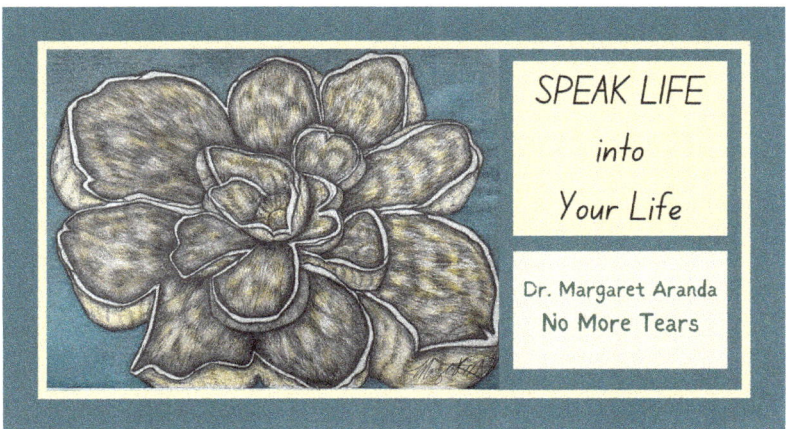

Speak healing.

Make plans for your new future.

There's one more step to do, and that is to *see yourself getting better.*

You can listen to my 10-minute podcast, SPEAK LIFE Into Your Life at https://DrMargaretAranda.Substack.com

Visualize Yourself Healed

To get through tough times, some people visualize themselves walking, working, and being with their children. For example, Holocaust survivors described exactly that: living for the future, detailing out plans and things they would do with their family.

One of the things I did to see myself better was, of course, to keep going from doctor to doctor until I finally had a diagnosis.

One survival trait I learned was to determine within 5 minutes if the doctor could either say, "I don't know" or "You're too complicated for me."

No one told me to exhaust the medical system. But if the doctor didn't know what I had, I kept "doctor-shopping". Only after seeing 24 doctors did I finally get a diagnosis of dysautonomia.

I came up with the idea the endocrinologist should run a particular test to evaluate whether I had diabetes insipidus. Both times, I was right—but I had to make the doctors think it was their idea to run the tests.

But what really helped me get out of bed, in addition to the medical solutions? The spiritual solution was not only to pray, but to see myself getting close to Christ, to see myself walking with him.

I did this in a very particular way that no one taught me to do. It started when I was crying. I couldn't stop; I was sobbing and getting short of breath. I felt destitute but not hopeless.

I tried to pop myself out of it by saying I was going to give myself 3 days or 72 hours to stop crying. So, I tried that once. It worked. Three days later, I pulled myself up by my bootstraps. And I stopped crying.

But then something else happened. Maybe I fell, or my PICC line got infected, or clotted. Or my battery ran out. Or everything happened at once.

I would find myself crying again. Because I could see the temptation to keep crying forever, I gave myself another three days to get over it.

This happened repeatedly, until one day while crying, I was also cold. It was dark and cold.

So, I imagined. I was at the bottom of a great dark, wet well.

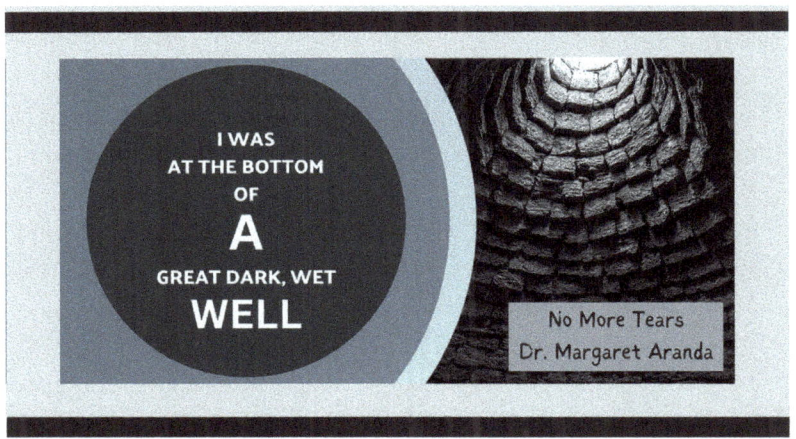

It was a deep well and I couldn't see much light at the top. Water was trickling down various intervals of the brick interior, and I could hear the "Drip, drop."

I stayed at the bottom of that well for three days. I let myself cry.

Then on the fourth day, I envisioned myself crawling and scratching to get at the top.

Like a mountain climber, I could hold on to the tiniest grooves.

LIKE A MOUNTAIN CLIMBER, I LEARNED HOW TO HOLD ON TO THE TINIEST GROOVES

No More Tears
Dr. Margaret Aranda

I learned how to hoist myself up.

Over time and after many falls to the bottom for three days each, I learned the route. And over and over again, I would fall again.

Until one day, I climbed high enough to see light. And I kept climbing to see a stick or something hanging into the well from outside, at the top. Then I fell again.

The next time I got up that high, I went a little higher. The stick began to move. Then it grew a hand.

Wait!

It *was* a hand!

It was a hand all along, and it was *the hand of Jesus.* He was reaching for me, and he wanted me to come out of the well.

I grabbed his hand, and he lifted me out.

I saw the most beautiful mountain scene, like the opening act of *The Sound of Music* with Julie Andrews. Just like her, I spread out my arms and gleefully twirled in a circle!

But then, something happened.

I don't remember exactly what it was, but there I was.

I was back down at the bottom of the well, crying again.

That only happened once.

The next time I made it to the top, I got out.

I see myself with Jesus every day, and I see the green hills and lambs. I continuously marvel at what a wonderful world our God has created for us to enjoy.

I marvel in it. And I'm never going back to the bottom of that well. Not ever again.

I envisioned I had to work to get well. And when I got well, I would never be that sick again.

And I vowed I would never go to the bottom of that well again.

Unfortunate Catastrophes

I wrote the first version of this book while still brain-injured, but I wanted to tell my story the right way for this version.

I think it is of value to describe some unfortunate things that happened to me, and other authors, at the hands of a particular publishing company for one of my previous books.

In the vanity model, a book publisher obtains startup money from the author. Then they publish the book and follow the terms of the contract, which should be detailed with events like book signings, audio books, and book trailers. They should market the book on their website and social media, perhaps even set up author interviews with newspapers.

My first book publisher was a big disappointment. After spending about $3000 to publish, there was a short-lived book trailer. But they did not even do a Facebook article or a Tweet about my book.

When I confronted them on it, no one could answer my email. This person was no longer there, and that person did not know anything about it. Weeks and months went by.

Then I opened the mail to find I got a check!

Excitedly, I opened it. My eyes blurred; I had to wipe them. It was unbelievable! The check was for three cents.

That happened maybe three times. Maybe the highest check was for seven cents.

Later, I found my book on other people's websites when I had the rights to it. I wrote letters to the sellers, called the website and still, other people have sold my books without my permission.

Over 12 years, I wrote 6 books from bed. All were by the same publisher. I was sick, too sick to notice my environment and happenings, but in time I saw that my publisher still was not marketing any of my books.

And it wasn't just me. It was other authors, too. They had also given their money to the same book publisher. Others reportedly kept paying for this and that, a book trailer or press release, or sent to do a book signing at remote places with no one there.

As it turns out, the book publisher went out of business. I am not sure how, but it turns out their state filed racketeering charges against them. They reportedly pleaded, "No Contest" to charges.

The state also gave us authors a chance to show that the company lost money for us. Unfortunately, only about one quarter of authors ever saw a cent from the state-mandated settlement.

I just kept paying them to publish five more books.

I was just one of thousands of authors. I was disabled and bedridden for twelve years, and had this first book been more of a financial success, it may have done many things for me.

It may have helped save my marriage from a man who wanted me to bring in an income. As it was, in time, my marriage was doomed. My friends were happy to come over to my house for big parties with free drinks while I was well. But they all left me to rot in bed.

Only a couple of people believed in me, and of those, most were paid to be my caregivers. But they stole from me. Boy, did they ever steal. I can't even talk about the big things they stole, but they also stole little things, like my beach towels, bras, baby clothes.

They stole my jewelry, my books, my credit card. They charged their tools, the neighbor's flooring, then charged the neighbor for the installation. I bought one caregiver with four children a van. She returned it behind on payments, with a huge dent in it from where her boyfriend kicked it in a rage.

By the time I woke up from twelve years of sickness, my financial life was a disaster. The divorce was settled without my having an attorney of record, the house was foreclosed upon, and I was charged income tax for money the caregivers received.

It was as if no one expected me to live.

My house was like a home goods store. People figured I would never know . . . but I did. And I do.

I remember sobbing to creditors. I couldn't even speak. I couldn't even defend myself. And when I tried to file a loss with the home insurance company, they dropped me because they thought I was lying about the thefts.

Christmas decorations were not missed until the next Christmas. No one used beach towels in the winter, so that was a good time to steal them. No one barbecued in the winter, so that was a good time to steal even the barbecue utensils.

Much later, I was approached by a media company to turn three of my books into a major network movie. They, too, wanted money up front again, and I said no.

How did the loss of potential income for my books affect my life? I'll never know what could have been, or what should have been.

I lost everything that the world holds precious: my marriage, my child, my home, my monthly income, my health, and my pride. Losing the ability to have income from my book was just another defeat in a sequence of unfortunate events.

I was just one of many authors who was ripped off by the publishing house. I never saw a penny of the settlement the publisher had to pay with the plea bargaining. One of many who, for some reason, did not deserve or earn the right to some small compensation, not even the money I put into it.

I wasn't going to let it make me angry and bitter.

I turned the negative into positive because that is what God does, and I knew he could do it through me and in me.

And I still believe that everything happens for a reason and that God can take all these negative occurrences and turn it into good.

Dysautonomia

What is dysautonomia? Dysautonomia or Postural Orthostatic Tachycardia Syndrome (POTS) is a dysfunction of the autonomic nervous system (ANS). The ANS controls automatic body functions that you cannot control: your heart rate, blood pressure, food digestion, urination and stool elimination, and more.

It was the reason why I needed to utilize the PICC line and the IV drip. Basically, I received this diagnosis due to two small strokes in my brain, which were sustained during or slowly evolved after the car accident.

When the ANS functions properly, your leg veins squeeze when you stand up. This allows blood to be redistributed to your brain, so you don't pass out.

With dysautonomia, you stand up and faint. If you come close to passing out but do not, everything can turn gray. This 'gray out' can repetitively occur, and little white spots can float around in the gray.

When the ANS does not function properly or automatically, you faint when you stand up. Food sits in your gut, and you feel full after very small meals. Or if you eat too much, you throw up. You may not feel like urinating for hours. But then when you go, you lose it all right away, and you can't get it all out. You may lose urine and become uncontrollably incontinent of both urine and stool and must wear adult undergarments. And it may be very embarrassing if you lose your bladder on a plane.

The loss of bladder function is called a "neurogenic bladder", wherein the bladder can't "feel" full or empty. The loss of gut motility is called "gastroparesis".

Both would magically heal.

No one prepares you for any of this. You gradually figure it out, or it never gets diagnosed so you go about life as best as you can. In that case, you know something is wrong, but no one can determine what it is. At best, you get a diagnosis and proper treatment. At worst, you are told you are pretending, and you are ridiculed, or worse.

As a child with dysautonomia, if all the doctors told your parents there was 'nothing wrong' with you, they would tend to believe the doctors. After all, they should know.

The Tilt Table Test

During my illness, the standard test was the tilt table test where I was placed on a hard table, then strapped with Velcro across my forehead, shoulders, hips and legs. Then they hooked me up to an EKG to look at my heart rate and rhythm.

Buzzz! Buzzz!

They slowly started lifting the table, so that I was 'standing' up. I could hear the technician asking me if I was okay. I didn't like him at all.

He had put my hospital gown on before the procedure, and he left my breast showing, which I did not like.

But I was strapped in, so I couldn't move. I was at his mercy, so I couldn't complain, either.

"I'm going to throw up."

He brought me the tiniest vomiting tray in the entire world, and I remembered thinking he would need five of them. That's the last thing that I remembered, other than my left breast was still showing and I still didn't like him.

Then the room turned quiet.

Quiet and dark gray.

My left ventricle was slapping its walls on itself because I had no systemic vascular resistance. There was no blood going into my heart, much less into my brain.

In rebellion, my autonomic nervous system was trying to get blood to my brain. It failed to do it by squeezing my leg veins to raise my blood pressure.

The only way my ANS could get blood to my brain was to increase my heart rate, so it tried. My heart rate shot up. But it didn't help; it was too late, too much of a loss.

I passed out for about twenty-two seconds.

When I woke up, there were five doctors staring? Down, peering into my face and yelling at me.

"Are you okay?"
"Margaret!"
"Margaret!"

They were shaking me. My eyes were open, but I could not speak. Their voices were far away. I heard one of them exclaim, "I've never seen anyone pass out during this test!"

I wanted to slap him.

But I could not move or talk. After a bit, though, I could move and speak. Slowly, my life's effervescence came back to me. My brain started functioning again.

They told me what happened.

My ex was standing in the room the whole time and saw everything. I don't remember him speaking a word to me. I don't remember him by my side when I woke up. His voice wasn't there.

After I sufficiently recovered and the doctors all left, I was alone. It was as if the show was over. I was vindicated, I was right, I wasn't pretending. Now they could all go home and talk about the spectacle of me that day.

I was embarrassed for myself. I guess I felt humiliated, like I was on display as an oddity. Abnormal. Different.

Later, when I heard my ex explaining to someone else what happened, he described by saying, "It was barbaric."

To prove I was sick, I had to faint. It wasn't just a "light faint" or a graceful one. It was a Herman-the-Munster, barbaric, and inhumane test.

Maybe it had to be done to shut everyone up, that I was not faking and what I had was real. I understand that today, the Tilt Table Test is obsolete in many hospitals. Maybe too many people died, I don't know. Maybe it was too barbaric. Maybe we're better than that now, and don't need to 'prove' the diagnosis in such a way.

Maybe now we just take the heart rate and blood pressure laying down, and then standing up. If the blood pressure goes down too much and/or the heart rate goes up too much, *boom.* You have dysautonomia. No need to force you to faint.

I am very grateful my cardiologist absolutely got my diagnosis, gave me the right treatment, and pointed me on the road to recovery. He put me in cardiac rehabilitation, where he implemented physical therapy with someone who knew to give me Jobst stockings and an abdominal binder which really helped me to stand up without fainting.

The stockings and binder squeezed everything below the waist, to keep blood from pooling when I stood up. It allowed me to have a better chance at not fainting.

I will forever be indebted to Dr. David S. Cannom for all he did.

Photo courtesy: Yelp   Photo courtesy: YouTube, Channel 7 News

When no one else did, Dr. Cannom believed in me. He was the one person in my life that trusted me, believed in me, had pure empathy and compassion for me, and helped me get better.

But it is very sad that some children with dysautonomia were treated much like animals, being left outside in a shed or abused because no one ever believed anything they said. Maybe if they had the tilt table test during childhood, their parents would have believed they were ill, and they would have helped their own child. It would have validated their illness.

In my case, I had my illness validated. Everyone knew I was legitimately sick, and I was not pretending a thing.

Or, so I thought.

My ex told the judge that I was faking it. Even though it is against the law in California, he stopped paying alimony because that's what the judge awarded him in the divorce. He allowed my case to settle without my having any legal representation at all. I had no lawyer of record with me in the final deposition; the court reporter did not even ask for my Driver's License or any other form of ID.

I lost my house, lost custody of my child, and only had scheduled visitation and received a relative pittance for alimony. I was bedridden with a brain injury, but I was ordered to have ten years of alimony and then to 'go back to work.'

Trusting God

I put my trust in God. In my trials, I gained internal mightiness in trusting my Lord. Mighty in the sense that God is in my life, and I am at his humble service. Mighty in the sense that I don't have to pray for this or for that. I only need to pray that God does what he wants with my life. I found that if I left the details up to him, that he would make all things work out for good.

With God's help, I would overcome any adversity.

Migraines

On a typical day, I woke up and threw up.

I opened my eyes and thanked God for another day. After several bouts of gagging and vomiting, some saliva from my stomach lands in a silver cylindrical trash can by my bed. I wiped my lips with a white tissue and watched as it fell onto the pile of pre-existing ones.

My eyelids were too heavy, and my chest felt sunken in. My eyes burned when I blinked, and another new diagnosis waited around each corner; this week, it was dry eyeballs.

My Kerlex was falling apart over where it covered my IV, and if I didn't get it changed soon, I would look like a homeless lady wearing tattered pieces of clothing.

Before this, I never had a migraine in my life. I saw patients in the ER who needed trays for their vomiting, and I worked with them over time . . . they needed ondansetron, pain medication, Phenergan, and a quiet, dark room with no lights. They were sensitive to loud noises and looked plainly miserable.

I knew what worked for my migraines, and it was usually hydromorphone 4 mg. One ER would call me a drug addict, and another would ask if I needed more. I never knew what to expect but when you are throwing up constantly, nothing mattered but stopping it.

Where was my dignity? If no one was going to keep my dignity, then I would have to keep it myself.

Dignity

It is difficult or impossible to maintain one's dignity in a hospital. The most consistent lack of dignity, no matter which hospital or ER, was shown by nurses who left me on a bedpan for hours at a time.

Prior to the diagnosis of diabetes insipidus (DI), I was urinating everything out that I drank, and more. By definition, DI causes "polydipsia" and "polyuria", increased thirst and increased urination.

But I could not drink enough to keep ahead of it, so I had to frequently urinate. I think they got tired of bringing me a bed pan, or they were too busy with everyone else, so accidently (or accidently-on-purpose), they *forgot about me*. I could not drink enough to keep ahead of it, so I had to frequently urinate. I think they got tired of bringing me a bed pan, or they were too busy with everyone else, so they either accidently, or accidently-on-purpose forgot about me.

The longest time I had to keep my buttocks up in the air, bridging my body over the urinal, was two hours. It was too full to move myself, or it would spill in my bed, and then I would be sitting in my own urine. That would make an even bigger mess for the nurses who would grow to resent me, so I couldn't move. I was at their very mercy.

During one of my hospitalizations, the charge nurse sat on my visitor's chair in my hospital room. It was 9:00 p.m. or so, and I was very tired at the end of the day. I had been admitted to the hospital by ambulance, as 911 had been called for chest pain. The chest pain felt exactly like uterine labor contractions: sharp, crushing, and squeezing. Suffocating.

I was scared. The normal tests were done to see if I had a myocardial infarction, (MI), AKA heart attack, with such as electrocardiogram (EKG) and blood tests.

Since I cannot run on a treadmill (with and EKG to detect signs of ischemia or infarct), I underwent the standard thallium stress test (the adenosine gave me a humungous headache) instead.

That night after the test, my regular nurse came in to dispense my medications. One was a beta-blocker used to slow the heart down and provide remodeling after a heart attack or myocardial infarction (MI). But wait! No one told me I had an MI, so why should I take the drug?

I wanted a doctor to look me in the eyes and tell me first.

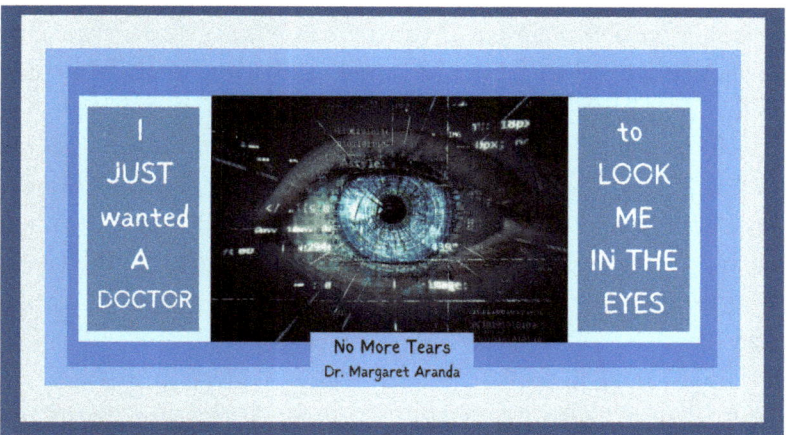

No More Tears
Dr. Margaret Aranda

That is the way that it is supposed to be done. I listened to her lecture me for literally twenty minutes.

I could not escape her. I was trapped, abused, jailed, and at her mercy. My 'fight or flight' response was highly activated, and my pupils were large, as if I was fighting a tiger. But I kept still. I kept my cool. That was the only thing I could do to preserve my own dignity.

When she left, my heart rested and I asked an orderly to get the Charge Nurse (they run the whole floor, supervising the nurses) to come into my room.

I explained to the Charge Nurse how upset I was because no one told me I had an MI, and I refused to take a heart-slowing agent until I discussed the matter with my doctor.

And then it happened again.

She said, *"You need to be the patient, not the doctor."*

I could not change *who I was*. Being a doctor wasn't a *profession*. It was *a life*. It permeated my being.

I sat calmly, again fuming on the inside. I let her have her say, and then I still refused to take the beta-blocker.

Little did either one of them know that my heart rate goes down to *35* beats per minute when I sleep at night. On admission to the ward, they always had to reset the Hewlett-Packard monitor alarm so that it only beeped if my heart rate was under 35.

I still refused to take the pill. She continued to demean me by lecturing me on how many decades she spent in this hospital. There was no argument and only silence from me. Another 20 minutes went by, and I wondered how they even had that much time to spend lecturing me in my room. I was on a cardiology floor and certainly other patients with real heart attacks needed care? It was more important to lecture me like I was in jail and just a child?

And no, I did not have a heart attack. It was spasm of the esophagus that felt like a uterine labor contraction, and it disappeared just as fast as it appeared, never to return.

On another occasion and unbeknownst to me, they discharged me from the hospital, yet no one told me. They let me reside overnight in my hospital bed with no apparent attending of record.

Everyone just ignored me.

Everyone
just
ignored
me.

No More Tears
Dr. Margaret Aranda

The office staff at Good Samaritan Hospital are beyond cordial and professional, and the hospital team was highly trained and professional beyond their years.

I was so grateful to God that eventually, we were led to cardiologist and dysautonomia expert, Dr. David Cannom.

Practicing Nursing

There were many dedicated nurses that treated me with respect and preserved my dignity. But our relationship was not always just that of nurse: patient; it was academic, that of pupil: teacher.

As an anesthesiologist, I learned how to draw blood in an undergraduate college phlebotomy course. At USC, I learned to draw blood by the Jail Ward window moonlight, because if the light was turned on, twenty men would wake up with everyone wanting something and suddenly, my sleep would go out the window for the entire night. So, I learned how to draw blood quickly and quietly in the dark, unobtrusively slipping in and out of a ward that was filled with sleeping patients. It was great practice because I didn't have to see a vein; I just had to feel it and know it was there. Like a blind person, my tactile sense magnified.

By the time I was a Stanford resident and Fellow, it was easy for me to "find a vein" and get blood out of the most difficult patients such as those on chemotherapy. It brought me great joy to put a fearful patient at ease by quickly and effortlessly popping in an IV, only for them to say, "It's already in? I didn't even feel it!" (I used lidocaine under the skin first, to numb it up.)

It was natural to me that during my twenty-one or so hospitalizations over the first two and a half years, it was my pleasure to return the favor of all the patients who let me practice on them, by letting nurses practice putting an IV in me.

The importance of learning for emergency situations and blood transfusions is paramount for any nurse, so I, upon admission, when they arrived to put in an IV, asked them if they wanted to practice putting a large 18-G needle in me.

Their response was always bordering on glee, because it presented itself as such an unusual but critical opportunity. The atmosphere would change. Suddenly, I wasn't just a patient; I was an anesthesiologist letting them turn the tables on me. I explained that it wouldn't be hard, I knew which vein to use, and I would walk them through it.

Recognizing the value of the offer, no one ever said no.

~ ~ ~ ~ ~

Age 48: Being a Pin Cushion

It was another emergency hospital admission, another ambulance in the driveway, another unknown period that I would be away from my home and my baby girl.

I told a nurse named Gloria that she could practice putting in an 18-G needle in my arm. We both knew I was dehydrated but she could not pass up my offer, so she went out to find a bigger needle.

When she returned, her face emanated the perfect balance of empathy and concern. As a newly employed nurse at the hospital, she appreciated this teaching opportunity beyond measure.

I never forgot her.

A year later, I was hospitalized again for dehydration. No one could get my vein to place an IV. I felt like a pin cushion and dreaded the thought of yet another nurse trying to put in my arm, as we were running out of veins.

Finally, I asked if they could call the on-call anesthesiologist to put in my IV.

Having to "call anesthesia" is a failure. It marked that the patient was an impossible stick, and no staff was capable of "getting the vein".

Invariably, the anesthesiologist would be treated like the lifesaver that she was and would further insult the staff by silently finding a vein in 5 minutes or less.

Elevating it from an RN to an MD standpoint said a lot. It was an embarrassing admission, and I knew it.

As a last-ditch effort before calling anesthesia, the nursing staff offered to search for their "best nurse" at putting in IVs.

After about 30 minutes, the same nurse came in to give me an announcement.

Lo and behold, guess who was going to try one last time on my IV?

It was Gloria, the same nurse that put that 18-G needle in me so long ago!

And she got my vein!

She was so excited, yet humble, at being the "star IV nurse."

I was grateful that God gave me back my favors and multiplied everything back to me.

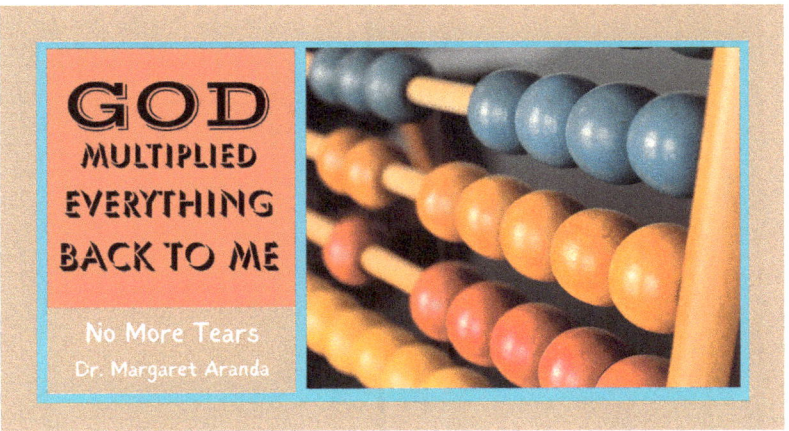

Falling

People fall. And when they fall, they can hit their head, or break an arm or a leg. Especially for elders, falling costs millions of dollars in medical and surgical care, as well as complications like bleeding, clotting, heart attacks, and medical errors.

For any disabled person, the institution of falling precautions is a goal. Prevention goes a long way because the avoidance of falling leads to a better quality of life.

That's because yearly, millions of people over age 65 fall, but less than half tell their doctor. And if you fall once, you double your chances of falling again.

Emergency departments treat falls about 3 million times a year; almost a fourth get hospitalized. Of those, about one third fracture a hip.

Traumatic brain injuries are primarily caused by falls.

Over 95% of all hip fractures are caused by falling, and not just a straight drop, but a sideways drop.

One in four adults aged 65 and older falls annually in the U.S., making falls, not heart attacks, the leading cause of both fatal and nonfatal injuries among older adults.

In 2020, the U.S. National Council on Aging reported that falls in older adults cost over $50 billion in medical costs, with an average hospitalization cost of $30,000 per fall.

And in 2021, the Journal of the American Geriatrics Society reported the prevalence of falls among older U.S. adults increased from 28.2% in 2011 to 31.5% in 2018, with the largest increase in those aged 85 and older.

The fear of falling is common for many people who fall, even if they are not injured. The fear causes some to lose interest in everyday physical activities, leading to muscle weakness and . . . an increased chance of falling.

"Falling" is a general medical word that can mean a variety of things. Our terminology should be more specific. Was it a gravity fall from a height? Or a trip and fall? Were there additional injuries sustained during the fall, like hitting the head?

The following definitions: may characterize a fall:

Fall
1. Low fall: from a bed, chair, or commode.
2. Medium fall: from a countertop or low ladder.
3. High fall: from a building, tall ladder, or mountain.

Trip and Tumble
1. Short trip: a trip on a carpet or small object at a low pace.
2. Medium trip: a missed step on a medium ladder or hill.
3. High trip: a missed step from a building, tall ladder.

Obstacles Hit on the Way Down
1. No obstacles hit.
2. Head: a hit on the head or neck.
3. Extremity: a hit on an extremity.
4. Torso: a hit on the chest or abdomen.
5. Back: a hit on the spine or pelvis.

Broken Skin
1. No broken skin.
2. Mild: superficial abrasion or laceration not requiring sutures.
3. Medium: laceration requiring less than 10 sutures.
4. Large: laceration requiring over 10 sutures.

Bone Fracture
1. No bone fractures or head/skull injury.
2. Mild: one bone fracture; no head or skull injury.
3. Medium: two bone fractures; no head or skull injury.
4. Large: over two bone fractures, no head or skull injury.

Head Injury
1. No head injury.
2. Mild: head injury without laceration or concussion.
3. Medium: head injury with laceration, no concussion.
4. Moderate: head injury with laceration and concussion.
5. Severe: head injury with laceration and concussion.

Blood Loss
1. No blood loss.
2. Mild: minimal blood loss under 1 ml/kg.
3. Medium: blood loss 1 – 3 ml/kg.
4. Moderate: blood loss over 4 ml/kg, no blood transfusion required.
5. Severe: blood loss with blood transfusion.

Vital Signs
1. Normal vital signs.
2. Mild: hypotension and heart rate 100 – 120 beats/min.
3. Medium: hypotension and heart rate 120 – 140 beats/min.
4. Moderate: hypotension and heart rate 140 – 160 beats/minute.
5. Severe: palpable hypotension and heart rate over 160 beats/min, abnormal rhythm, or cardiac arrest.

Fall Prevention

1. **Vitamin D.** For those over age 50, it is important to evaluate your risk of not only falls, but vitamin D deficiency that may lead to a propensity of bone fracture upon a fall, as well as overall COVID mortality.

   Studies show that having a blood level of vitamin D that is over 50 ng/ml is associated with a 0% chance of dying from COVID-19. A level of 20 is rickets, a bone strength deficiency originally found in children of the Industrial Revolution who worked in darkness and grew demineralized with defective bone growth.

   Attain a vitamin D level over 50 mg/ml. Talk to your doctor.

2. **Vision.** Prioritize an annual vision check with changes in eyeglasses, as needed.

   If you like to regularly do an outdoor exercise like walking, wear a pair of distance lenses, so you have no lower bifocal or progressive lens that may interfere with objects that may seem closer or farther than what they really are.

3. **Long-term Care.** If your job offers it, consider long-term care disability insurance that will reimburse you for approved caregiver needs and/or a nursing home. Or pay privately. The earlier in life that you obtain these services, generally the lower your initial premiums will be and the better your coverage will also be. We happened to do that, and we are very grateful that all the caregiver costs are not borne by us alone. And remember that caregivers can easily steal from you, especially if you are bed bound.

4. **Respond.** Do not overreact. Some people use that as a lifetime motto. Don't move if you have fallen and are in pain. But if

you can, try to get to a chair. Hoist yourself up onto the seat first; wait for help.

5. **Call for Help.** Have some methods of calling for help. For some people, this may be a phone number to call; for others, it may be a formal, paid service and a necklace tag that one pushes to call for help.

6. **Modify your Landscape.** Obtain a fall-free area of cushioning in case of another fall and/or a bedrail to help prevent falls. If you fall once, chances are you will do it again. Get rid of obstacles that are common causes of trips and falls, like clutter, dog or baby toys, and rugs lying on the floor.

   Provide disability-safe surroundings for use daily: shower chair, shower and commode grab bars, bed rail, stair rails, added light or brighter light bulbs, and avoid using a step stool. Use non-slip mats on the shower floor and bathtubs.

7. **Caregiver.** A caregiver aids with moving, lifting, shopping, going to the restroom, preparing meals and any activities of daily living, or ADLs (see Appendix for ADLs). Family may provide caregiving; if not possible, they may financially contribute to finance a caregiver.

8. **Home Health Nursing (HHN).** As fast as possible, recover from a fall. After a fall, medical insurance may pay for home health nursing visits two or three times per week.

9. **Exercise.** Do whatever you can, and institute bed exercises if you are bedridden, have lower extremity weakness, or balance difficulties. The stronger your core strength and arms, the more you will be able to minimize injury on the way down and the more durable your body will withstand a fall.

Yoga and Tai Chi help make legs stronger, increase core strength, and improve balance.

10. **Medications.** Sedatives, opioids, and antidepressants can cause drowsiness, affect balance, and your response catching yourself.

11. **Foot Pain or Poor Footwear.** Some elders need to change shoes with shoelaces for those having Velcro straps instead. Avoid flip-flops or clogs, and wear shoes with support or insoles. Take the extra time to purchase appropriate footwear.

If you did not sustain injury on your first fall, you may not be so lucky on the second fall. If you fall once, prevent another fall.

The Gift of Prophecy

Throughout the Old Testament, there are references to prophets like Elijah and Moses. Their prophecies included future events like the city where the Messiah would come from and particulars about how he would die.

Some non-Christian religions are known to accept that Christ was a prophet, and there have been exceedingly many lectures on the conundrum of Christ's being a prophet versus what exactly Christ preached and, to that end, who he really was.

To accept that he was a prophet and that he preached that he was the Son of God, or so it goes, means that one has to accept one of three things: (1) that Christ told the truth, (2) that Christ was a liar, or (3) that Christ was deluded or deranged.

To the logical brain, many scientific studies on Christ's life that have sought to quantify the prophecies that were said of the Messiah versus those that were fulfilled in this one-man Jesus of Nazareth. The chance that during his lifetime, this Jesus of Nazareth did fulfill the many prophecies of the Old Testament has a statistical significance that is almost incomprehensible.

Essentially, it is figuratively equivalent to filling the state of Texas two miles high with quarters, painting one of them blue, mixing it up, and then picking out the blue one on the first chance. This mathematic logic has led many otherwise skeptics to accept Christ as who he said he was, the Son of God.

Even as Christ left the earth, he told the disciples that he was not leaving them alone. He was leaving them with the Holy Spirit. He also described that some people would have special gifts and some, the gift of prophecy, the gift of hospitality, and more.

Prophecies are words of wisdom that are revealed from God through the Holy Spirit, and into the prophet or prophetess. It is "a still, small voice." The accuracy and truths of the Prophetess bear witness to the gift.

God gave me the gift of prophecy. I believe it helped me during my pain clinic, to know my patients' diagnoses. I also believe it helped me handle over 2,500 patients during the plandemic, to know what they needed to prevent or treat COVID.

It began when I unexpectedly went to a prayer group meeting, and the pastor had words of prophecy for me. First, he clarified to the eight or nine Christians gathered around me that we had never met, that he had no knowledge of me or my past; I acknowledged these truths:

1. **Previous Neck Injury.** He then laid out my then recent life and said this was not the first time I had hurt my neck. I told the group that I had been assaulted by a patient before and had sustained a severe neck injury and, ten years later, had a neck surgery.

2. **Lots of People Around Me.** Before, there were just a few people coming and going to our home. Now, people surrounded us as workers remodeled the backyard and family visiting to help care for me and our daughter.

3. **God would send people to our home.** We were not to be fearful of being taken advantage of. We were to help these people. I told the group that because of the car accident, our home was already altered, being visited by a variety of medical professionals, caregivers.

4. **God would heal me 100%.** He would heal my body so that I could be a testimony. I promptly accepted complete healing, having faith in God's word spoken through this man.

5. **God would give me the gift of the Holy Spirit.** I would be a prophetess. I did not know what this would entail, but I accepted it. It was understood that I was to be a witness and spread the gospel of Christ, teach and lead people to Christ, and give God the glory for being so close to my heart.

6. **God would give me dreams.** And my dreams would have meaning. At rare intervals, I do have vivid dreams and I try to search for their meaning.

    For example, I for years as a child, I would have nightmares that my father died. And then he was the first person in our family to die.

I still search for the meanings in my dreams, and like David, I wait for God to speak to me in this way.

7. **God allowed the car accident to happen.** I would have a change in my direction. On this one, I didn't know why I could not have just sustained a broken leg or some other common malady, so I figured I must have a hard head. I was meant to learn and grow.

    Maybe it was meant to be that my father with Alzheimer's would not need me to care for him anymore. He died six months after our accident. But perhaps God thought that I had already paid my dues (and would continue doing so on his deathbed). I knew God was getting me ready for my own quest, but I didn't know what it would be, so I just tried my best to forge onward and forward.

My future direction would naturally come to pass. I would know my road because it would become obvious to me.

During my multiple hospitalizations, many nurses, doctors, and other professional caregivers told me that I should write a book.

I lost sleep every night and had lots of awake bedtime, so my fingers started doing the clicking on the keypad.

Even today, as I type one sentence, the next sentence is already in my head. Sometimes, a noun presents itself and I think to myself, "That's a good word" as if it didn't come from me.

Usually when I write a book, it doesn't take long. It comes to me in a wave, like a flow, and I *need* to *get it out* of my system, as if it is a song. I write from morning to night, then from night to morning, sometimes writing until the wee hours.

In this way, it feels like God gives me the words, the paragraphs, and the chapters.

I edit as I go along, so that any corrections in spelling or grammar are corrected as they are made. Today, I have 115 pages written, and today is day three. I feel like this book will be done by Sunday, so it will have taken me six days. This, to me, is a gift of prophecy in that my words ring true to your ears.

God doesn't always talk to us in predictable ways.

GOD DOESN'T ALWAYS TALK TO US IN PREDICTABLE WAYS

No More Tears
Dr. Margaret Aranda

One day when I was really sick, I had three caregivers in my home at the same time. Suddenly, I had them line up.

I don't know why, but I needed them to do this. As they stood shoulder-to-shoulder in line, I had an impression, a still small whisper that made me yell.

"One of you is pregnant or is about to be pregnant!
You are NOT supposed to get an abortion!"

Everyone denied it. No one was pregnant. I told them to go home and check.

Sure enough, one of my caregivers was pregnant, but she didn't tell me until a month later.

She was sitting with her boyfriend in an abortion clinic, and the nurse had just stood in the doorway holding her chart. She called her name.

When she called her name, my caregiver ran.

She ran outside and down the street. She told me that she remembered everything I spoke. She could hear my voice *telling* her not to go inside.

She had a beautiful boy, who must be about 15 years of age by now.

One morning, I awakened in the hospital to see a very petite, little lady sweeping my room. I watched as she glided the wide brown broom briskly along the waxed wood floor; her movements were so smooth. She had short dark-brown hair and the Holy Spirit spoke to me again, in his still, small voice. He told me that,

1. This nice lady looked a lot younger than she really was,
2. She had been working here in the hospital for many years, and
3. She had a son or sons that she had much sorrow over. It tortured her, and this self-torture was unnecessary.

A feeling of panic, of urgency, came out of my mouth. I began to continuously pull on my caregiver's arm, telling her to translate to this little lady in Spanish. I said,

> "Hurry! I must talk to her right now! God is giving
> me a word for her! I need to talk to her."

Meekly, the little lady, whose name I never knew, came back over to the hospital bed. Her back was disfigured with thoracic lordosis with the backbone vertebrae around the shoulders hunching her over, so she looked like she was looking at the ground when she walked. In my mind, it reminded me of the way I too needed to walk when my blood pressure was low, hunched over.

> *"You raised your son the way he should go, and you did*
> *the best that you could. He makes his own decisions and*
> *has his own mind. You are not responsible any longer.*
> *Only pray for him. Pray for him every day."*

Humbly, the little lady verified that these words had true meaning to her. She did have a son, who was thirty-three years old, and a situation over her son had been heavy on her heart . . . She said she did not feel that she was a successful mother.

But once she heard the words of the Holy Spirit, she was alleviated of her silent sufferings and encouraged by how closely God was involved with her and her life.

Dangers of Lying in Bed

Being bedridden carries the risk of several complications, many of which are important in this era of COVID-19 and lung disease.

Atelectasis. Lying down changes the lungs such that they do not inhale or exhale as much while standing. This leads to collapse of the alveoli at their bases, near the abdomen.

How can you tell if you have atelectasis? If you happen to have a pulse oximeter in your home, you can put it on your finger and check your % oxygenation.

A normal oxygen saturation is about 97-99%. If you have chronic obstructive pulmonary disease (COPD), you may have a 'normal' of 94-96%.

If you have healthy lungs but get sick with COVID-19, your oxygen saturation can dip from 97% to 92% just from spending a lot of time in bed. The easiest way to determine if your 92% is "real" is to follow this exercise:

1. Take 3 slow, deep breaths.
2. Hold the last breath for 30 seconds.
3. Wait about 10 seconds before re-reading the pulse oximeter and see if it goes up.
4. If it goes back to normal, you had atelectasis. Spend more time out of bed, take big breaths more often, or better yet, go on a walk if you can.

5. If it doesn't go back to normal, it may be a "real" value that needs further medical attention, like a pneumonia or sleep apnea.

Pneumonia. Once collapse of the airways occurs, these areas may be susceptible to pneumonia. Once pneumonia hits a disabled or able person, there is an increased risk of death, which is why pneumonia has been dubbed, "an old man's best friend" because it hastens death.

Your doctor may need you to be sitting up in bed, dangling your feet. This allows your alveoli to open, preventing pneumonia and increasing your lung capacity. Getting out of bed and sitting in a bedside chair also opens up your lungs.

The more you move around, even if you are ill, the better it is for your lungs.

If you have had pneumonia once, you may always be susceptible to having it again, and you need to take special precautions to be sure and minimize any complications to your lungs.

Pneumonia and Asthma. If you also have reactive airway disease or asthma, any irritation or process can trigger bronchoconstriction, or a closure of airways. Use special care to be sure you always have an inhaler, and if you are additionally allergic to bee stings or have had anaphylaxis in the past (i.e., lip, tongue, airway swelling), be sure you always have an EpiPen® with you.

An EpiPen® provides epinephrine to counteract the allergic reaction. It may come in the form of an injectable needle that goes into a muscle like the thigh. If it does not work the first time, you may sometimes use *the opposite thigh* for a second try. Never use the same spot twice, because the first one decreases the blood supply to the area, and the second injection won't absorb into the blood stream.

Sleep Apnea. Has anyone ever told you that you snore? If you snore and are also overweight, there is a good chance that you may have obstructive sleep apnea (OSA). It is more likely to occur in the obese.

Obstruction occurs when you fall asleep, and the back of the tongue blocks your back airway, preventing oxygen from going in or out of the lungs. This is usually associated with a downward dip in your pulse oximeter reading to the low 90s and is definitely not normal.

Additionally, the obstruction causes apnea or a halt in breathing. Holding your breath after obstructing, especially while sleeping, is dangerous and may cause death.

The good news is that the fix is as easy as wearing a mask overnight and getting better sleep because of it. If you have medical insurance, your primary care doctor can refer you to the pulmonary department for a sleep study.

You pick up a device in the pulmonary department that studies lungs, wear it overnight at home, and then return it so it can be read. The department goes over your results with you, and if your results are consistent with OSA, you are prescribed a breathing machine to take home and use each night.

The machine operates exactly like a ventilator, with settings for those who are breathing normally. It provides positive pressure (i.e., the machine blows air into your lungs with a bit of force) when you initiate a breath, opening your lungs more than usual. Then when you exhale, it prevents you from closing your lungs all the way, stenting open the alveoli. This prevents them from collapsing all the way down when you are in between breaths. That is, it prevents atelectasis by providing continuous positive airway pressure (CPAP).

CPAP masks used to be extremely uncomfortable and tight-fitting. The machine used to be so loud that spouses could not sleep, and now they are much more user-friendly. If you have a CPAP machine, you essentially have a ventilator in your home.

Atrial fibrillation or Afib. If you are over age 40, your risk of developing AFib is one in four. Having Afib means you are *five times* more likely to have a stroke than if you didn't have Afib.

The reason why AFib causes brain clots is because it first leads to abnormal heart beats, then abnormal flow, with pockets of inert blood that can form a clot. The clot can dislodge from the heart and go to the brain, causing a stroke. To prevent this, patients are placed on a blood thinner.

You can calculate your personal stroke risk of Afib by using an AFib calculator.

An AFib calculator uses risk factors for stroke in those who already have Afib. Factors include age, sex, previous history of blood clot, heart failure, heart attack, peripheral arterial disease, a replacement heart valve, and other factors to determine personal risk.

The best scenario is to get rid of the AFib so that you neither worry about getting a clot nor bleeding due to atrial fibrillation or blood thinners, respectfully.

AFib and Obstructive Sleep Apnea (OSA). If you go into AFib, it may be that you first had OSA as a contributing factor.

Never get cardioverted or a cardiac ablation procedure without being evaluated for obstructive sleep apnea. Use your CPAP machine for 3 months before a procedure to eliminate A-fib. That is because you have a much higher chance of success the first time, if you keep wearing your CPAP! And after cardioversion or a cardiac ablation, keep wearing your CPAP mask to keep that AFib from coming back!

If you are over age 50 and your heart rate is in the 90's, that is not normal. If you ran down the street, your heart rate may jump up to 140 beats per minute, and then *Whoosh!* Suddenly, you must stop because something is wrong.

You cannot get a full breath of air and you feel your heart palpitating or beating too fast, kind of fluttery. Call 911 or go to the ER. You may have atrial fibrillation and require a heart rate more like 55 beats per minute. Usually this is done with a beta-blocker medication that slows it down and if you are one of the blessed ones, your heart rate will slow and the atrial fibrillation will "cardiovert" on its own, without those shock pads zapping your heart (like you see on TV).

Hypoxia. A big hallmark of COVID-19 lung disease can make the oxygen saturation go way down, into the 91-94% range. This means there is a low and borderline dangerous level of oxygen in the bloodstream.

If the saturation goes down to 88%, most agree that it is time to consider going to the hospital. However, today we must worry about "Hospital Protocols" that may cause kidney failure or death, i.e., the use of Remdesivir (also known as Veklury). Remember that we never treat "the numbers" – we treat the patient. So, if your oxygen saturation is low and you feel fine, that is completely different than if you do not feel well. Some may need a chest x-ray to look for pneumonia, and insurance covers an Urgent Care visit so that one may still avoid a hospital emergency room just to get a chest x-ray.

In this regard, see what happened to Grace Schara, a 19-year-old with Down Syndrome who was hospitalized and eventually over sedated. Then she stopped breathing. The doctors forced a "Do

Not Resuscitate" or DNR on her, despite having no permission – and despite the family screaming that she was NOT a DNR. Her father Scott has the landmark lawsuit that is taking the Catholic-run hospital and its medical staff to court for her death. Please visit OurAmazingGrace.net

Most medical freedom doctors advise all their patients to avoid the hospital at all costs. Do not let a loved one stay alone in a hospital. Ask questions, take notes. Visit COVID protocols that are on the internet, and see our handout for COVID care at https://bit.ly/COVIDCareWithTracker

If your chest x-ray is normal with a low oxygen saturation, one may get a CT angiogram to check for lung clots, or pulmonary embolism. Doctors may check for clot formation and heart attacks by checking blood labs like D-dimers and troponins, respectively.

Spirometer. The doctor may want you to use a spirometer machine to stent your alveoli open. It is a plastic device with a little ball in it; when you breathe in, the ball rises upward.

It provides "incentive" and turns lung exercises sort of into a game, by promoting opened alveoli. Your doctor would write an order for an incentive spirometer and frequent exercises are performed.

In hospitalized or ICU patients, we encouraged use of the spirometer during each TV commercial watched. Family can serve as cheerleaders for children and loved ones who need encouragement using the spirometer.

Breathing is important, and so is the avoidance of under-breathing, especially during sleep.

Maneuvers to Improve Oxygenation. A helpful maneuver that improves lung oxygen is simply to lay prone, on your stomach. It allows gravity to divert the lung blood flow to the front of the chest, allowing the smallest alveoli to better exchange oxygen. We do this in the ICU for patients on ventilators who are not oxygenating well, and it works at home.

Another helpful maneuver for those who are coughing productive sputum is to have the patient lie on one side. Then a helper can pat the back from the bottom to the top, over and over again as if mowing a lawn. It loosens mucus, so be prepared with a tissue.

Reanimation

Upon awakening, I tried to slow down the rush of awareness. I tried to feel each stimulation of neurons in my brain and in my spinal cord. I slowed my own reanimation as much as I could, harnessing the energy of that initial bolus of electrical energy from a little knob to the entirety of my brain.

I listened for the sound of birds. Their chirping told me I was still alive.

After a few moments, I could hear finches or crows in the trees. As my eyes slowly and deliberately opened, I praised the Lord aloud for another day, as if it were a present with endless possibilities.

Inside, I began to muster up whatever life and energy that I could muster up. My reanimation changed to joy at the prospect of making it to live another day.

I sat at our master bedroom window seat every morning. I sang out to the Lord at the top of my voice, "Holy, Holy, Holy." Birds arrived. Squirrels gathered. To God. To hear Praises of our Lord and Savior.

I watched the garden, the hummingbirds, and the flowers. I counted each day as a blessing. I glorified God at the top of my lungs, and I was filled with the Holy Spirit.

Every morning, upon awakening, I sang. First my eyes opened, then I listened for birds. I created five minutes to glorify and praise God.

These were my moments of reanimation, of spinal cord and brain stimulation, and of a great 'reset' that changed my way of thinking.

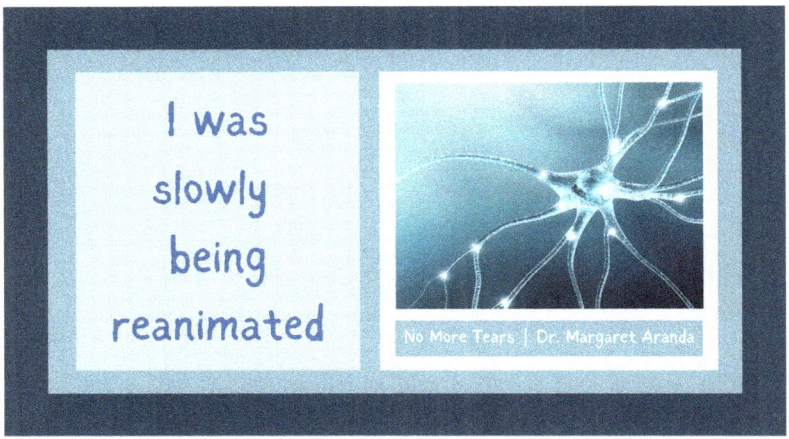

I could feel my neurons being activated.

Traumatic Brain Injury (TBI)

I started my professional interest in TBI as a medical student.

By the time I was an anesthesiology resident, I participated in a drug trial that was for getting patients out of severe cases of TBI. It was for refractory brain swelling after head injury, and all the usual tools failed to alleviate the brain swelling.

When I presented my research at a doctor's professional meeting, it was felt to be "too controversial," and I did not even receive a third-place prize for my presentation.

Later, the very same research was published as a *Rapid Communication* in the journal, *Neurosurgery*. Apparently, other doctors had the same idea we had regarding the research and felt that this new use of a drug could possibly save lives.

Unfortunately, it did not, and we had proven it by detailing the research in *Neurosurgery*. They were kind enough to communicate this to all by publishing our research via the fastest route then available, a *Rapid Communication*.

I'm sure that this publication prevented future deaths, and it is my opinion that it was important information that should have been fully appreciated when it was first presented.

Little did I know that one day, I would suffer a TBI.

During my brain testing, I would forget what the day of the week it was, the date, and the last three words I was supposed to remember. I could not remember what someone told me to do; my brain fog was too thick to think. I couldn't remember the easiest things. I relearned how to speak, cook, do laundry, and how to think.

I had no history of hitting my head at all, and this made it harder for doctors to give me a traumatic brain injury (TBI) diagnosis.

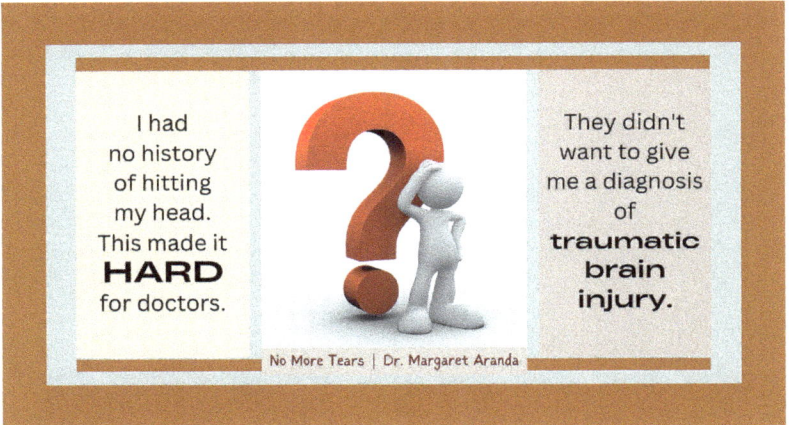

The first symptoms that can alert you to a potentially major head injury is sleep. And sleep. Vomiting and nausea are bad signs and practically necessitate an MRI scan of the brain.

I did not know I had a brain injury until I had figured it out for myself. I had gone north instead of south on the 405 Freeway, on my way to pick up someone at the airport. I never do that. I was lost. I knew which way to go but it was like I stared numbly while driving, as if I wasn't there at all. It was as if someone else was driving.

I think everyone with a TBI thinks about death because they lost part of their brain. It's an organ, and the body senses that loss as if a leg was lost. It changes hormones, mood, and abilities. It puts one in a fragile stupor.

My inabilities bothered me, but I was too brain-injured to know how unable I was. "I" was inside "me," but it was a blunted "me," a different version of "me" and I didn't know who I was.

As I got better, I found more joy in things I remembered liking. I loved to swim and being in the water made me feel like more of "myself" than anything else. It was as if I was one with the water, like a fish. It was comfortable. I fit in, with no judgement or expectation.

Water allowed me to enjoy myself, my body.

I REMEMBERED HOW MUCH I LOVED TO DO LAPS

No More Tears | Dr. Margaret Aranda

It triggered enkephalins and endorphins, like the "runner's high." I think that helped the pathways in my brain that were used when I swam . . . it somehow made dendritic astrocytes repair or help repair my neurons.

I know they teach us in medical school that neurons cannot replicate themselves. But if Jesus Christ made a blind man see, isn't that nerve tissue? The optic nerve is . . . a nerve. But it isn't just *any* nerve. It communicates directly with the brain, so it is brain tissue.

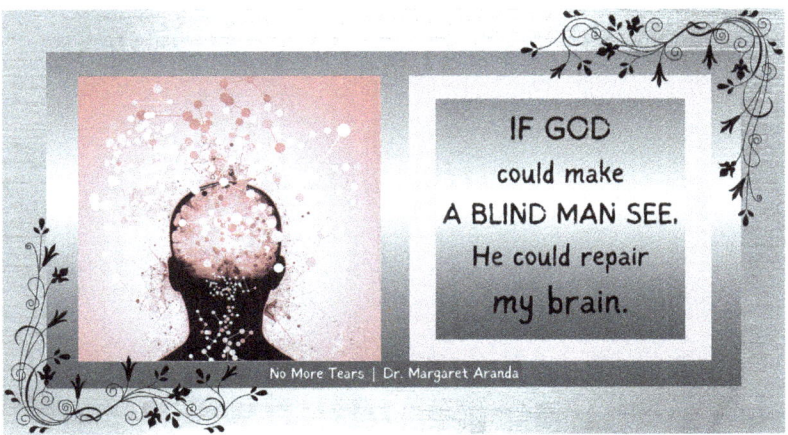

IF GOD
could make
A BLIND MAN SEE.
He could repair
my brain.

No More Tears | Dr. Margaret Aranda

My neurons had to replicate themselves or grow new ones out of nothing but his breath, his light, or his word. I had to reinvent myself. Because God was reinventing my brain.

I was subject to anxiety and depression at times, but I never wanted to kill myself. I wanted to live, but it was harder than I ever imagined.

Dying scared me. I wasn't ready to die, so *that* scared me more. In time, I learned that living was harder than dying, because at least there was no 'end' to it . . . the days kept repeating themselves.

I kept scratching and clawing at the walls of the well. Whether it was learning to sit in a wheelchair or learning to walk or say "the," everything was like climbing out of that same well.

So, I kept climbing.

Whatever it was, I put my mind to complete it. I looked up secrets of success and discovered how to implement them in a meaningful way. Most of them had to do with motivation.

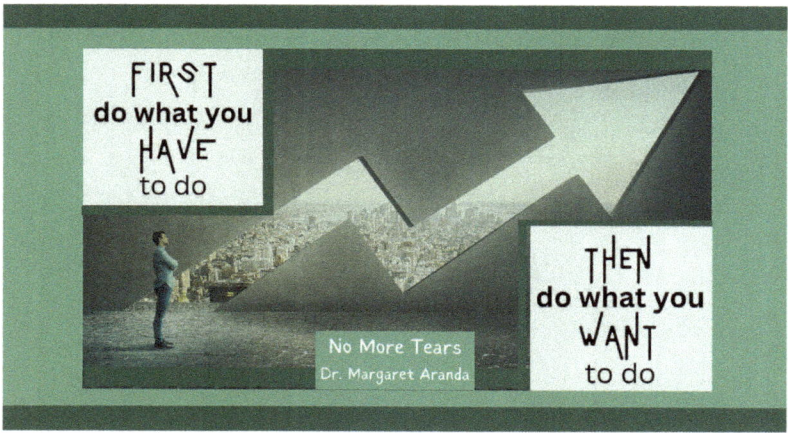

My Top 11 Tips for Success

1. I can do all things through Christ, who strengthens me.
2. Do the things I *have* to do first, then do the things I *want* to do.
3. Keep solving a problem, no matter how long it takes.
4. I don't have to be the smartest person; I just have to be the one that never gives up.
5. Nothing good comes without effort.
6. Effort is never useless.
7. I am getting better each day, even if I don't feel like it.
8. Don't rely on my feelings; rely on God.
9. Perseverance cannot be taught. I have it, and it is my gift.
10. Do not rely on my own understanding. Rely on God's promises, his Word.
11. If I have a one-in-a-million chance of walking again, I AM that one-in-a-million person!

I didn't want to die. Dying would separate me from my daughter, and I had to be there for her.

Living was work. It was tiresome, took energy and effort, and had so many unknowns and multiplicities of problems.

But once I decided to live or knew that I *would live*, my attitude changed. I had to be strong. No matter what, I *would be* strong.

When I stopped my fear of dying, I began living.

Eternal Faith

Hebrews 11:7

> By faith Noah, when warned about things not seen, in holy fear built an ark to save his family. By this faith he condemned the world and became heir of the righteousness that is in keeping with faith.

How stupid they must have thought Noah was during the time he was building the ark. The Bible teaches us that he was the laughingstock of the town.

He was prepared to lose family and friends to follow God's instruction. We must be willing to do the same.

Noah's dedication and faith created an eternal future.

Noah created his own heaven on earth, and he saved the lives of his family and mankind. How much he trusted God.

How do we trust God? How do we exercise faith?

Matthew 6:25-28

> Therefore, I tell you, do not worry about your life, what you will eat or drink; or worry about your body, what you will wear. Is not life more than food, and the body more than clothes?
>
> Look at the birds of the air: they do not sow or reap or store away in barns, and yet your heavenly Father feeds them. Are you not much more valuable than they?

Can any of you by worrying add a single hour to your life?

And why do you worry about clothes? See how the flowers of the field grow. They do not labor or spin.

Matthew 6:34

Therefore, do not worry about tomorrow, for tomorrow will worry about itself. Each day has enough trouble of its own.

Luke 12:23

Then Jesus said to his disciples: "Therefore I tell you, do not worry about your life, what you will eat; or about your body, what you will wear.

For life is more than food, and the body more than clothes."

1 Corinthians 9:24-25

Do you not know that in a race all the runners run, but only one gets the prize? Run in such a way as to get the prize.

Everyone who competes in the games, trains with strict discipline. They do it for a crown that is perishable, but we do it for a crown that is imperishable . . .

2 Corinthians 4:18:

So, we fix our eyes not on what is seen, but on what is unseen. For what is seen is temporary, but what is unseen is eternal.

James 2:21-22:

> Was not our father Abraham justified by what he did when he offered his son Isaac on the altar? You see that his faith and his actions were working together, and his faith was made complete by what he did.

2 Thessalonians 1:4

> That is why we boast among God's churches about your perseverance and faith in the face of all the persecution and affliction you are enduring.

1 Timothy 6:12

> Fight the good fight of faith. Take hold of the eternal life to which you were called when you made your good confession in the presence of many witnesses.

Hebrews 3:14

> For we are made partakers of Christ, if we hold the beginning of our confidence steadfast unto the end.

Hebrews 6:12

That you may not become sluggish but imitate those who through faith and patience inherit the promises.

Hebrews 10:39

But we are not of those who shrink back and are destroyed, but of those who have faith and preserve their souls.

Hebrews 11:1

Now faith is the substance of things hoped for, the evidence of things not seen.

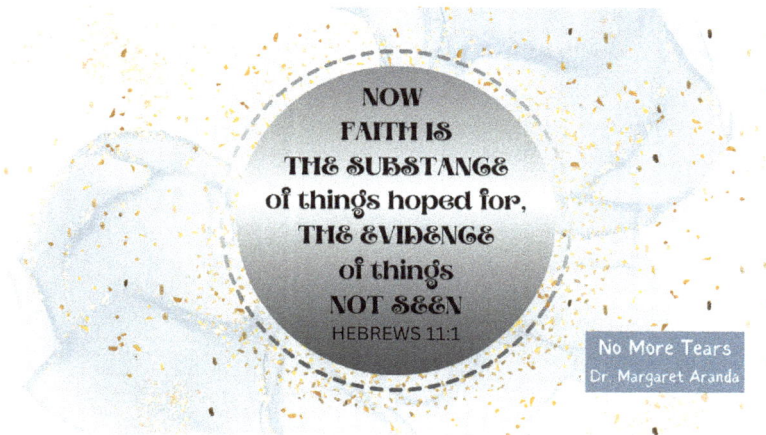

Hebrews 11:11

And by faith even Sarah, who was past childbearing age, was enabled to bear children because she considered him faithful who had made the promise.

Hebrews 13:7

Remember your leaders who spoke the word of God to you. Consider the outcome of their way of life and imitate their faith.

Exercising our faith takes perseverance and a fight. But God did not leave us defenseless. Instead, he gave us not only his armor, but his own full armor.

Ephesians 6:10
Finally, be strong in the Lord and in His mighty power. Put on the full armor of God, so that you can make your stand against the devil's schemes. For our struggle is not against flesh and blood, but against the rulers, against the authorities, against the powers of this world's darkness, and against the spiritual forces of evil in the heavenly realms.

Therefore, take up the full armor of God, so that when the day of evil comes, you will be able to stand your ground, and having done everything, to stand. Stand firm then, with the belt of truth buckled around your waist, with the breastplate of righteousness arrayed, and with your feet fitted with the readiness of the gospel of peace. In addition to all this, take up the shield of faith, with which you can extinguish all the flaming arrows of the evil one. And take the helmet of salvation and the sword of the Spirit, which is the word of God.

Pray in the Spirit at all times, with every kind of prayer and petition. To this end, stay alert with all perseverance in your prayers for all the saints. Pray also for me, that whenever I open my mouth, words may be given me so that I will boldly make known the mystery of the gospel, for which I am an ambassador in chains. Pray that I may proclaim it fearlessly, as I should.

Spouses

About four years after the first version of this book was written, I entered a writing contest by Anthology, for a Monkey Star Press article.

~ ~ ~ ~ ~ ~ ~ ~ ~ ~

Age 55: I Had It All

It was in December of 2015, and I had been in bed still, exercises rolling around in my head, filling me with dread . . . and then I checked my email.

Well, what do you know? It was an email from Monkey Star Press, regarding my submission for a short story about "Moms and the Holidays." After all submissions were given a scenario of "the Holidays," the person of interest was to be the Mom. And that was it!

My story was completely fictional, derived at a time when I was at Stanford doing extra years of post-doctoral training in anesthesiology and critical care. Everyone seemed to have someone, and there was a Christmas dance.

It was accepted!

Attached was a five-page book contract to be a contributing author in a holiday book. I focused with all my might to scan each page, sign it, and then return it to the editor. My intent was to get it right the first time, and not stick out as being different than anyone else.

My focus and concentration were still off. No, just Shhh! Let me do this! Ah! Ah! Wait! I am al . . . most . . . done . . . and I don't want to get mixed up again . . . what page was I on? Uhm . . . ok, the last page now . . . OK! It is done. Now . . . Now we can talk.

"Mom as the center of attention for the Holidays" . . . let me see . . .

There was no family waiting for me when I came home from the hospital. Not on my birthday, Thanksgiving, nor the Holidays, including Christmas. Then New Year's Eve arrived and there wasn't anyone to kiss, not for 30 years, being single all through my 30s and 50s. Alas, just when I got used to not being 'a couple' again, Valentine's Day came around and slapped me in the face . . . ah, but I digress and for this story, I wanted to write a happy story, one that seemed to escape my personal experience.

My home was quiet, and the night of the writing, I remembered the girl next door fell asleep with her music super loud until two o'clock in the morning. This wasn't in the story, but when I called the police for a well check on her, they had to climb into her bathroom window to get in her house.

Then next morning, she told me that I saved her life because she drank too much alcohol and needed her stomach pumped out or she would have died from an overdose of alcohol!

With that thought, I created a story of her and me . . . two women who had a dream of a happy Holiday family.

I made up a story.

I reminisced like as child who knows the smell of chocolate chip cookies in the oven, or like a dog who hears food being poured out and already beginning to salivate from across the room.

Pavlovian, yes. Automatic.

This story pervaded my being. My goal was to trick myself into thinking that I could have had it all.

In my dream, I was 40.

As I wrote, I took my feelings from deep down inside, knowing that I still yearned for the same dream. It never left.

I painted the best picture of the most memorable times, and filled in the blanks, the missing parts, with my imagination of what I would have liked to have had waiting for me at home.

The effervescence was that of a house that was 'just messy enough,' filled with just 'the right amount of laughter.' In the background, the dog chased the cat, someone lost a shoe, and romantic, symphonic hard rock floated in the air, wisping whisps of whispers in my ear.

I would turn around to an arm around my waist, and my husband, who I adored like no other, would grant me a good, long kiss.

He would take me into his strong arms and without so much as a single word, he would make the rest of the workday disappear, much like a magician pulling a bunny out of a hat.

He was tall and burly, smart and romantic, and seemed to live to make me smile and laugh, to offer a genuine distraction away from all mundane things of the world, and onward to the higher spiritual calling that we both shared.

And together, we would get lost in this world, our children gazing as we laughed and played, fully clothed on our bed.

And they would shrink back in that innocent glee, thinking to themselves,

"They're at it again. Let's go play outside!"

And just before they wrapped their bodies around the doorway, they would take one long, last look at us. And smile. And be comforted knowing that no matter what, we would always be there for them.

And as the children walked away, they had no idea that we were imprinting their future families inside their little brains, their future spouses and yet-to-be-begotten children, and yes, even their future pets.

And I would smile a hearty grin, for surely there was nothing better than being a mother and a wife, for the entirety of my life.

I was grateful for the ability to write this story, because today, I have everything.

~ ~ ~ ~ ~ ~ ~ ~ ~ ~

I found everything in Ed, who is my best friend and my royal ally, my protector and my man.

What the Bible Says About Love

Love is not easily offended, and we have been instructed to love one another as Christ has loved us. We also have specific instructions for spouses, how they are to behave with one another in a Christian household.

1 Corinthians 13

> If I speak in the tongues of men and of angels, but have not love, I am only a ringing gong or a clanging cymbal. If I have the gift of prophecy and can fathom all mysteries and all knowledge, and if I have absolute faith so as to move mountains, but have not love, I am nothing. If I give all I possess to the poor and exult in the surrender of my body, but have not love, I gain nothing.

Love is patient, love is kind. It does not envy, it does not boast, it is not proud. It is not rude, it is not self-seeking, it is not easily angered, it keeps no account of wrongs. Love takes no pleasure in evil but rejoices in the truth. It bears all things, believes all things, hopes all things, endures all things.

Love never fails.

But where there are prophecies, they will cease; where there are tongues, they will be restrained; where there is knowledge, it will be dismissed. For we know in part, and we prophesy in part, but when the perfect comes, the partial passes away.

When I was a child, I talked like a child, I thought like a child, I reasoned like a child. When I became a man, I set aside childish ways. Now we see but a dim reflection as in a mirror; then we shall see face to face. Now I know in part; then I shall know fully, even as I am fully known.

And now these three remain: faith, hope, and love; but the greatest of these is love.

Ephesians 4:31:

> Get rid of all bitterness, rage, and anger, outcry and slander, along with every form of malice.

Ephesians 4:32:

> Be kind and tenderhearted to one another, forgiving each other as in Christ, God forgave you.

Ephesians 5:

> Follow God's example, therefore, as dearly loved children and walk in the way of love, just as Christ loved us and gave himself up for us as a fragrant offering and sacrifice to God.

But among you there must not be even a hint of sexual immorality, or of any kind of impurity, or of greed, because these are improper for God's holy people. Nor should there be obscenity, foolish talk or coarse joking, which are out of place, but rather thanksgiving. For of this you can be sure: No immoral, impure or greedy person—such a person is an idolater—has any inheritance in the kingdom of Christ and of God. Let no one deceive you with empty words, for because of such things God's wrath comes on those who are disobedient. Therefore, do not be partners with them.

For you were once darkness, but now you are light in the Lord. Live as children of light (for the fruit of the light consists in all goodness, righteousness and truth) and find out what pleases the Lord.

Ephesians 5:21-33

Submit to one another out of reverence for Christ. Wives, submit to your husbands as to the Lord. For the husband is the head of the wife as Christ is the head of the church, His body, of which He is the Savior. Now as the church submits to Christ, so also wives should submit to their husbands in everything.

Husbands, love your wives, just as Christ loved the church and gave Himself up for her to sanctify her, cleansing her by the washing with water through the word, and to present her to Himself as a glorious church, without stain or wrinkle or any such blemish, but holy and blameless.

In the same way, husbands ought to love their wives as their own bodies. He who loves his wife loves himself. Indeed, no one ever hated his own body, but he nourishes and cherishes it, just as Christ does the church. For we are members of His body.

"For this reason, a man will leave his father and mother and be united to his wife, and the two will become one flesh." This mystery is profound, but I am speaking about Christ and the church. Nevertheless, each one of you also must love his wife as he loves himself, and the wife must respect her husband.

Colossians 3:12

Therefore, as the elect of God, holy and beloved, clothe yourselves with hearts of compassion, kindness, humility, gentleness, and patience.

Colossians 3:18-19

Wives, submit to your husbands, as is fitting in the Lord. Husbands, love your wives and do not be harsh with them. Children, obey your parents in everything, for this is pleasing to the Lord.

Colossians 3:21

Fathers, provoke not your children to anger, lest they be discouraged.

Galatians 5:22

> But the fruit of the Spirit is love, joy, peace, patience, kindness, goodness, faithfulness.

1 Peter 1:15

> But as he which has called you is holy, so be you holy in all manner of conversation

1 Peter 3:1-2

> Wives, in the same way, submit yourselves to your husbands, so that even if they refuse to believe the word, they will be won over without words by the behavior of their wives when they see the purity and reverence of your lives.

1 Peter 3:7

> Husbands, in the same way, treat your wives with consideration as a delicate vessel, and with honor as fellow heirs of the gracious gift of life, so that your prayers will not be hindered.

Philippians 4:8

> Finally, brothers and sisters, whatever is true, whatever is noble, whatever is right, whatever is pure, whatever is lovely, whatever is admirable—if anything is excellent or praiseworthy—think about such things.

Proverbs 17:19

> Whoever conceals an offense promotes love, but he who brings it up, separates friends.

The Importance of the Bible

The Bible was my guide, my salvation and my cure. God's love was my friend, my source of comfort and inspiration. I could go to him anytime I wanted, just like you can, by just closing my eyes.

Better than Dorothy and the Wizard of Oz, I did not even have to click my heels three times.

I could be with God
Just
by
closing my eyes
and
wishing
for
him

No More Tears
Dr. Margaret Aranda

I always had the power within me to create my miracle, but it took me twelve years to learn to rise, stand, and have a halfway normal life.

Many people ask me what I have done since recovering. What did God heal me for? His kingdom, my children, and society. Who have I helped? Many more than I would have thought or prayed for, many more who showed gratitude.

What would have happened if I had died?

Pain Management for
Spinal Cord Injury

Age 58: A Sign from God

When I learned that Jennifer took her life in fear of living without pain management, I googled her doctors' name exactly in this manner:

"Dr. Forest Tennant and Phone Number"

To my surprise, I didn't see a display showing the number of hits nor how many seconds it took to display them, like normally happens when you google anything.

Instead, my computer screen was all black but for two giant, white lines that said,

"DR FOREST TENNANT" and underneath was:
"555-286-0833"

Both his name and phone number were huge, filling up the page.

No More Tears | Dr. Margaret Aranda

That never happens when you Google someone's name, so my first thought was,

"God, you must be talking to me. I think I'm supposed to call him."

I immediately called him, and he returned the call, inviting me to go into his clinic the next day.

No doctor had come forward to volunteer to continue his clinic, probably because no one wanted to prescribe high-dose opioids to a clinic of 150 patients. The "opioid crisis," which was really an "illicit fentanyl crisis", was at its height, and it carried all the stigma.

On my first day, he showed me a huge chart about 6 inches thick and introduced me to the patient, who had a basketball-sized tumor in her right abdomen. Then he showed me the other five charts she accumulated over the last 20 years. I read them all and told him I was done and ready to see the next patient.

He said, "What? I didn't scare you yet?"

I smiled and knew this was going to work for me.

At USC, I had reviewed "bjillions" of big charts, and they did not intimidate me. I told myself that if I just kept everyone on the same things they got last month, at least I wouldn't kill them.

As it turned out, I set my sights too low at that time and God blessed nearly everyone who stayed in clinic with improvement. Many went down on their opioids and were able to seek pain management near their homes with a local doctor. For me, that was the ultimate compliment that I did a good job.

As an anesthesiologist, I was intrigued with the wide array of laboratory blood work and medications that Dr. Tennant implemented as a public health and endocrinology expert.

For three months, I didn't change anything. Then I started instituting my own interventions, putting everyone in the clinic on the same thing at the same time. I collated all the entire medications everyone was on and tried everyone on everything.

I was familiar with many pain medications, but not everything. Quickly, I learned that most patients had Ehlers-Danlos Syndrome. I used Dr. Tennant's wealth of knowledge, collated it, and comprised a "Low Back Pain Protocol", published in my seventh book now available on Amazon, "Guidebook to Low Back Pain: Diagnosis and Treatment".

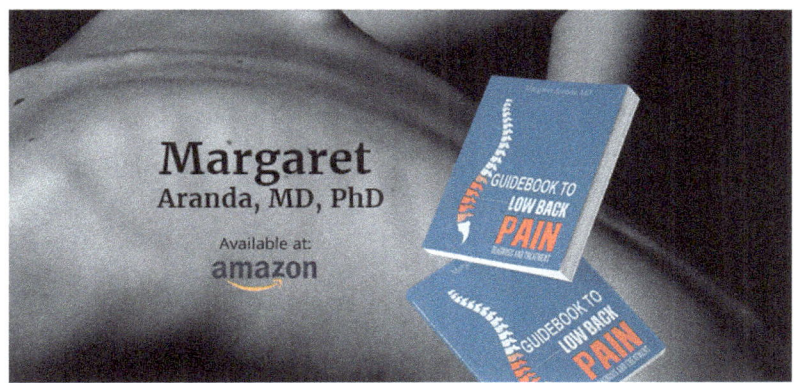

I believe God wanted this clinic to be saved from patient abandonment. Had I not assumed this clinic, some more of these patients would have taken their own lives.

Then the pandemic hit.

COVID-19

Suddenly, everyone knew what the disabled knew for so long: what it was like to be homebound, restricted, unable to go out and do normal things. It was a crash course in survival and some families did worse. Un-like mine, others did better.

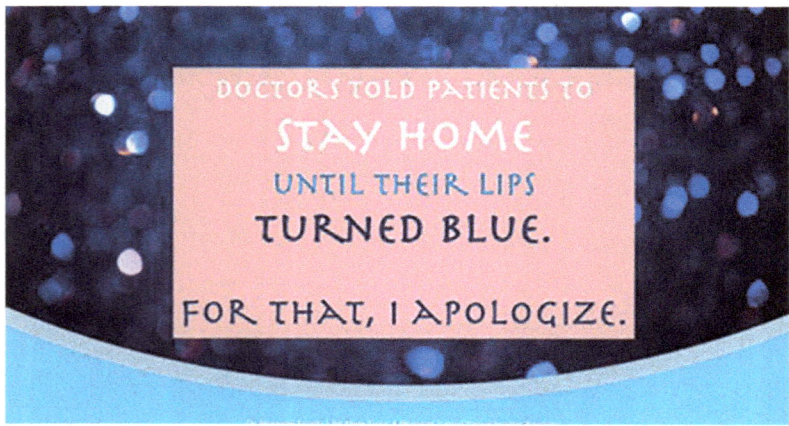

DOCTORS TOLD PATIENTS TO **STAY HOME** UNTIL THEIR LIPS **TURNED BLUE.**

FOR THAT, I APOLOGIZE.

I do not say the following lightly, nor do I mean to upset you, but I am compelled to state what I saw over the COVID years, how things were for those of us who tried to save lives.

I realize that what I am about to say is upsetting. If you have not yet come to these realizations on your own or through family or friends, I hope you keep an open mind and just listen to what I have to say.

The reason I say this is because I almost died. I almost wasn't here to save lives. I almost wasn't here to write this book and tell you what I know, what I saw, and what I did. This is the most horrific thing I saw:

No longer did doctors run to patients. They walked away.

No More Tears | Dr. Margaret Aranda

Violating the Hippocratic oath, doctors told patients to stay home until their lips turned blue. 911 Emergency Medical Technicians arrived and left without care, leaving my elderly patient on the floor. They told her there was "nothing" the hospital could do.

And when they did go to the hospital, patients were given Remdesivir (also known as Veklury), fluid overloaded, given shots without permission and under anesthesia, starved, denied visitors, wrist-restrained with cuffs in bed, without informed consent, sedated, anesthetized (see the story of Grace Schara at https://ouramazinggrace. net and https://ouramazinggrace.substack.com), and murdered for hospital reimbursement money, as high as $500,000 per patient.

Hospitals received money from the government for patients who died with certain criteria. The more patients who died in the hospital, I am very sorry to say, the more money the hospitals received. Hospital CEOs, Chiefs of Staff, Medical Directors, and Ethics Committees should all hang their heads in shame.

Lies of COVID deaths and COVID pneumonia were placed on death certificates, to make everyone think COVID killed, instead of intentional euthanasia by hospitals.

The Federation of Medical Boards sent a letter to doctors, telling of license reprisal should we prescribe ivermectin. That is when many of us knew there was something very wrong about what our country was doing to our people.

Your local pharmacist took on the role of God, with permission from the Pharmacy Boards, to deny filling prescriptions for ivermectin or hydroxychloroquine. In the beginning, I personally yelled at every pharmacist who refused to dispense ivermectin or hydroxychloroquine, as they knew that denial could kill my patients. I kept searching for proper medications, and no patient did without, especially after I found some ethical, private compounding pharmacists who made my job easy.

I thank God for our small, mom-and-pop pharmacies – support them however you can. You need to know that your neighborhood compounding pharmacist saved America's ability to obtain lifesaving medications, stock supplements, and provide nasal sprays and mouthwash. They are the heroes and heroines who helped us save millions of lives.

Prior to the Emergency Use Authorization for COVID-19 vaccines, school closures, masks, and vaccine mandates, the lack of sunshine and school socialization led to a rash of child suicides as young as ages 6 to 8. This was suppressed by our government, and they kept reinforcing the mandates.

As death rates falsely went up, governments ramped up the need for COVID-19 vaccines, *which had been researched for 20 years by Dr. Fauci's own statement*, patented and licensed with the hope of not reviewing adverse events for 75 years, i.e., "The Pfizer Documents".

The world was tricked into needing gene therapy biowarfare that alters the immune system, agents handled by the Department of Defense (DOD) as "vaccines". The CDC, FDA, and NIH were completely out of this loop. The world was tricked into thinking a vaccine would help death rates, transmission, or recurrence – it helped none.

Virtually every one of the following failed you, the public: the government, medical schools, the Federation of State Medical Boards, all State Medical Boards, the Department Chair of medical departments of all specialties, the American Board Certification programs, Deans of medical schools, doctors who did not promote COVID prevention or early treatment and/or who got paid per shot conversation or shot conversion rate, cardiologists and pathologists who saw blood clots and myocarditis and said nothing, obstetricians and gynecologists who saw miscarriages, infant heart attacks, fetal malformations, infertility, postmenopausal bleeding, and oncologists and family doctors who saw "turbo cancers" presenting in the final stages, when tumor spread to multiple body parts.

Hospital Chiefs of Staff, Chief Medical Officers, and Medical Directors received millions and billions of dollars in payment for promoting hospital killing protocols, which are still in action.

There is no ICD-10 Code for post-COVID vaccine *injury*, but there are a bunch of codes for refusing to have a shot, or not having had one. For example, there is no insurance code for "myocarditis related after a COVID-19 vaccine". The governments do not track vaccine injury.

To those who participated in legalized Remdesivir or Veklury euthanasia in hospitals to the tune of 1,000 deaths per day in the U.S. and continuing, but keep their mouths shut – you failed the world and need to ask for forgiveness. Those in the ICU who continued to intubate and ventilate patients when the death toll was higher for them, or who purposely sedated and anesthetized patients, causing respiratory depression and then withholding CPR – you murdered patients in cold blood.

I apologize to the public for all the failures of medicine. The conundrum of medical insurance, big pharma, and monetizing death has never been more self-revealing and disgusting.

Some sections of state or federal governments did not fail their people, like Uttar Pradesh and Mexico.

To help you with COVID Care and hospitalizations, if needed, please see the appendices for prevention and early COVID treatment, as well as Medical Directives for hospital instructions to the doctors and nurses. Includes additional resources like the Hospital Hostage Hotline, at protocolkills.com or 888-C19-EMER. GraithCare helps as a hospital and insurance advocate, at graithcare.com or 469-864-7149.

Thanks to all the doctors who were outspoken from the beginning. They taught the rest of us how to save lives, and to those who chose to pursue this righteous path despite income loss, targeting by medical boards, elimination of board certification, and personal sacrifices.

We knew what we were doing – keeping our Oath before God, and not man.

For that, I apologize. It violates the Hippocratic oath. Emergency Medical Technicians called via 911 refused to take patients to the hospital, saying there was "nothing they would or could do." I apologize for that, too.

It was difficult for me to know how to either prevent or treat COVID-19; no traditional national organization was helpful, not the CDC, NIH, FDA, or any other ABC group. Were doctors really that stupid with all those years of education that no one could recommend *anything* but wearing a mask and staying away from people? How could we accept such mediocrity?

Thank goodness my patient's husband told me about ivermectin, and the Frontline COVID-19 Critical Care Alliance at FLCCC.net.

When I saw Dr. Pierre Kory's passionate pleas to the US Senate Committee on ivermectin and success of the I-MASK+ Protocol, I was transformed. This doctor was a *real doctor.*

Without otherwise learning how to treat, I implemented the I-MASK+ Protocol and practiced COVID prevention and the early treatment of mild symptoms. Cold turkey.

I was honest; no one I knew had ever prescribed like this but the doctors that developed the protocol. I learned how to save lives from their piece of paper and from the pharmacists that dispensed ivermectin. They taught me everything I know.

A very special word about the contributions of Dr. Vladimir Zelenko and his Zelenko Protocol using hydroxychloroquine, zinc and azithromycin, and countless others who showed bravery by being lifesavers extraordinaire. Many, like me, were targeted, censored, and were forced to surrender their licenses. Still more lost their Board Certifications.

Without the entire FLCCC team who got the word out to the rest of us, so many doctors would not have known what to do for COVID-19 prevention or early treatment of early symptoms.

Thousands of patients later, there were bumps along the way, and two of our patients passed away in hospitals, reportedly after receiving Remdesivir against their explicit wishes.

None of our patients died at home.

Everyone lived.

Clearly, God brought me back to save them. There were doctors, nurses, firefighters, police, government officials, mothers, fathers, grandparents, adult children, and neighbors that were sent to us. We helped everyone we could.

But don't think that just because I could do it that your doctor should have been able to do it. Most prescribe their own repertoire of medications that are specialty-dependent, so they generally prescribe the same drugs all the time.

Rarely do all doctors have to learn how to use a collection of new drugs, but that is what a bunch of us did. We did it cold turkey. And we did it to save lives – because none of us could bear to tell people to stay home until their lips turned blue.

We knew that we were better than that.

Being an anesthesiologist was a tremendous help during the pandemic because we all had to learn how to prescribe drugs we had never used before. And the experience of prescribing for Dr. Tennant's spinal cord injury clinic put me at ease with using safe, everyday drugs I had never used before.

But that was something all anesthesiologists are comfortable with, because after all we had to train to give potent intravenous drugs in the operating room: muscle paralyzers, sedatives, antibiotics, reversal agents, anti-nausea drugs, diuretics, IV fluids, blood transfusions, and more. We literally put patients in a coma and then reanimated them.

Anesthesiologists master all body systems: the heart, lungs, kidneys, liver, and brain. They are experts in cardiology, pulmonology, urology, hepatology, neurosurgery, and neurology, resuscitating patients from exsanguination, respiratory and cardiac distress. As ICU doctors, they additionally are experts in long-term ventilation, pressor therapy, infections, trauma, resuscitation, and multiple organ dysfunction.

We had some patients with scary medical histories like having just one lung after cancer, or kidney transplantation. Some patients came to us on Day 1-2; others came on Day 16.

Plenty of patients were put on the I-MASK+ Protocol, which is now split into the I-Prevent and the I-CARE Protocols and can be found at https://flccc.net.

I now write at Substack, at https://theRebelPatient.Substack.com

I'm not the only doctor who can say this,

"All of our non-hospitalized patients survived COVID-19."

"No one died at home."

The only two patients who passed were in the hospital, unable to continue my care. Both got Remdesivir.

Natural Therapies

There are numerous natural therapies that I support, and they undergo constant updates. For explanations and more information, visit:

https://arandamdenterprises.com and https://renewandrefresh. substack.com:

Augmented NAC:
https://augmentedNAC.com/en 10% OFF CODE = HAHG4P

Best Lean Life and Lean for Good®:
https://bestleanlife.com/cb/?hop=draranda

Cortexi® Health for Hearing:
https://trycortexi.com/c/order-now.php?hop=draranda

LifeWave® Wearable Technology Patch
https://lifewave.com/margaretaranda

Metagenics™ Supplements:
https://margaretaranda.metagenics.com

The Good Inside SUPER GREEN and PROTEIN Powders:
https://155484.thegoodinside.com/

Zeolite Solution:
CLEAN SLATE®: https://therootbrands.com/dra

And

Touchstone Essentials®:
https://155484.thegoodinside.com/

Current Activities

While it is outside the purview of this book to relay what I learned over the last three years, here are three areas that have consumed much of my daily writings and sentiments:

SPEAK LIFE Into Your Life Podcast. To share my lessons learned, please join me for *SPEAK LIFE Into Your Life* podcast: https://drmargaretaranda.substack.com.

My Renew and Refresh Blog is is https://RenewAndRefresh.Substack.com. This site forms the introduction to my newest book on spike protein detox.

The Rebel Patient Blog goes over COVID-related and geopolitical issues of our time, including the World Economic Forum, Gates, the World Health Organization, 15-minute cities, and more: https://therebelpatient.substack.com

My most popular products can be found on our website: https://arandamdenterprises.com

My Rumble, most current interview with Ob/Gyn Dr. James Thorp: Landmark paper on COVID-19 vaccines – Pregnancy Outcomes. March 30, 2023. https://rumble.com/v2fs5iy-dr.-james-thorp-landmark-paper-on-covid-19-vaccines-pregnancy-outcomes.html

My Favorite Prayer for You

I speak life into your life, health into your bones and tissues, and blessings for a sound and strong mind that withstands the wiles of the evil one. I ask your doctors and nurses to have great insight on your diagnosis and treatment.

I order every medication you take to work better than intended.

I empower you to be healed of any wound or sickness, because God is no respecter of persons and if he healed me, he can heal you.

Believe God's promises, accept his healing. See yourself well, speak life into your life, and revel in his power and love.

Let him create in you a new man or woman, one with a peaceful mind and full confidence to persevere beyond that which you are able.

You have God's promises and his power.

Fight to live.

Live.

Persevere.

Don't give up.

Don't ever give up.

See yourself well.

Speak life.

God's Revenge

I could have been angry and resentful.
I could have blamed God for my problems.
I could have wallowed in self-pity.
I could have asked him to take down my enemies.

It would have made me bitter.
It would have made me resent God.
It would have taken away my joy.
It would have been my own idea of revenge.

Instead,

I gave my natural reactions to God.
I took everything as being in his will.
I rose above my feelings.
I gave him his own revenge.

And he

Kept me beautiful inside.
Continued to draw me close to him.
Lifted me up.
Gave me back more than what I lost.

So, I wouldn't do anything differently.

An Update On
Dr. Margaret Aranda

On October 18, 2011, Dr. Margaret Aranda-Ferrante received the Perseverance Award from the Invisible Disabilities Association (IDA) at **InvisibleDisabilities.org.** Her dream of meeting Founder Wayne and Sherrie Connell came true.

Since the writing of the original book, she now serves as Vice Chair of IDA. She is especially proud to promotes the National Disability ID, which can be worn at stores or airports to show others that someone with an invisible disability may need help.

You can:

1.   Order a personal National Disability ID Card here: **https://invisibledisabilities.org/national-disability-id/national-disability-id-card/** or

2. Donate to help launch a National Disability ID in your state here:https://invisibledisabilities.org/national-disability-id/

3. Visit Dr. Margaret Aranda Ferrante's Board Member Profile with the Invisible Disabilities® Association (IDA) here: https://invisibledisabilities.org/about/leadership/board-of-directors/dr-margaret-ferrante-board-member-bio/

4. Become an IDA Friend, including Gamers Support via Tiltify, Streamlabs, and Donating Cryptocurrency, Give in Memory, Create a Fundraising Page, or Give in Honor, Mail, or Text "GIVEIDA" to 44321: https://invisibledisabilities.org/support-ida/

5. Mail IDA Donations to:

Invisible Disabilities Association
PO Box 4067
Parker, CO 80134

Dr. Aranda works to increase awareness of Long COVID, Chronic Fatigue Syndrome/Myalgic Encephalomyelitis (CFS/ME), and post-vaccine injury, as well as to increase awareness of spikopathy and spike protein detoxification. She loves applying alternative medicine practices to traditional or allopathic medicine standards.

During her bedridden years, Dr. Aranda wrote six books and became a website designer and social media influencer.

On June 5, Dr. Aranda surrendered her medical license to the Medical Board of California. Her trip to the post office was filmed LIVE by Adam King on The Adam King Show:

https://madmaxworld.tv/watch?id=647e383c492826dd9ddfa1dc

You may see that Dr. Andrew Zywiec lovingly started a Give.Send. Go. for Dr. Margaret Aranda here:

https://www.givesendgo.com/arandaMD

Her voice may be soft, but her words are universal. They touch patients, families, friends, and they offer continued encouragement.

Appendix A – Memories

David S. Cannom, M.D., FACC, FHRS and Margaret
Aranda Ferrante, MD, during one hospital stay at Good
Samaritan Hospital, 4th Floor, Cardiology Suite.

In 1985, Dr Margaret Aranda receives a plaque in recognition for "Fine Guidance and Leadership" for three years of service on The Pre-Med Club at Sepulveda VA Medical Center in Sepulveda, CA. From left to right: Julie Seidl, Member, The Pre-Med Club; Faith Rothburn, Voluntary Services Department Chief; Margaret Aranda, Pre-Med Student; Harry Mannis, MD, Assistant Chief of Staff; Pamela Nagami, MD, Staff Physician; Wiley Barker, MD, Chief of Staff; Harvey Schneir, MD, Staff Physician, and Hiro Mori, Acting President, The Pre-Med Club.

Sepulveda
Veteran's
Administration
Medical Center
Red Cross
Blood Drive

No More Tears
Dr. Margaret Aranda

1982 Red Cross Blood Drive at Sepulveda VA Medical Center in Sepulveda, CA. Ronald L. Nelson, Director of the VA Medical Center, signs a card for blood donation for Margaret Aranda (left), President of The Pre-Med Club. Mattie Bierbower, Chair of the Employees Blood Drive, and Aubrey Payne, Field Representative, look on.

Almost 30 years later, in 2021, Dr. Margaret Aranda was Interim Chief of Anesthesiology at the Philadelphia Veteran's Administration Medical Center and Assistant Professor at the University of Pennsylvania, with Mr. Ronald L. Nelson as Hospital Director.

The real Little Missy Two-Shoes at two years old, just prior to her two-year-old birthday and the writing of Little Missy Two-Shoes Likes a Ladybug. She made every woman in the grocery store want to run home and tell their husband they wanted to try again for a baby girl. She had a vocabulary of over 100 words and loved to chit chat about anything. She loved to play Teacher and bake cakes. Most of all, she loved horses and started riding lessons. She had no fear of giant horses and spent hours grooming them.

From the Ladybug Party birthday cakes, we won 2ⁿᵈ Place at a local fiesta. This is a red velvet cake baked in a common oven-proof bowl. Chocolate frosting, red sugar granules, and Oreo Cookie eyes and spots! Served on a plate of arugula, accented by red sugar granules.

The real Little Missy Two-Shoes, transformed to cartoon character.

She was a perfect baby, lively, sassy, and smart. She loved animals, especially her bunnies, her horse, and her puppy. Since the time she could barely speak, she begged for a pet puppy. When we finally got her a puppy after two years of begging, she was a beautiful chocolate lab. Missy and Ella were both in the car accident with me and survived untouched.

Missy and Ella were both in the car accident with Dr. Margaret Aranda, and survived untouched, thanks be to God. At the time, Dr. Aranda was using a walker and had a continuous IV in her arm.

Toddlers get to know Little Missy Two-Shoes as they turn 2 years old and acquire an affinity for ladybugs.

Order ladybugs from your local nursery and let them out during any wonderful summer party for kids! And as they depart, they can hold their first biology book in their hands!

As they first adore Little Missy Two-Shoes and learn to like ladybugs, it is an easy transition to teach preschoolers how to cope with going to school. Perfect for first-time toddlers going to preschool, or those after-vacation and after-summer times when they transition to back-to-school times.

Little Missy started off all blue to go to school, but she learns all the new things she gets to do, and learns to love School, just like Little Missy Two-Shoes.

In 2012, Dr. Aranda did her first book signing of 2012 and won the Invisible Disabilities Association's Perseverance Award. YouTube: https://youtube.com/watch?v=A9RC_fPSbB0&t=10s

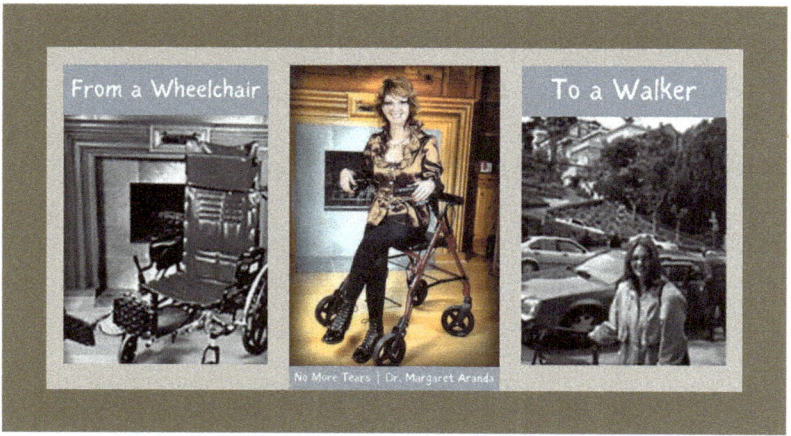

Above: Going from a wheelchair to a walker was wonderful. *Below*: While bedridden, Dr. Margaret Aranda became a licensed chaplain and ministered to a South African orphanage.

Appendix B – List of Medications and Supplements

DRUG	DOSE	FREQUENCY	DOCTOR
Metoprolol	25 mg	Twice a day	Dr. Ela Smith 123 1st St Sunshine, OK 999-232-5555
Ivermectin	11 mg	Twice a week	Dr. Gloria Tulane 356 Main Street Parktown, NC 876-373-5555
Spironolactone	100 mg	Once a day	Dr. Tulane

SUPPLEMENT	DOSE	FREQUENCY
Vitamin D	50,000 IU	Once a week
Vitamin C	2000 mg	Once a day
Zinc	30 mg	Once a day
Quercetin	250 mg	Once a day
Melatonin	6 mg	At dusk

Appendix C –
List of Recent Procedures

If you see many doctors and have had many surgeries or procedures, make a list like this for your doctors.

Surgeries/Procedures

1. March 2010: C5,6 Spinal Fusion: John Lem, MD (313) 555-5678. Santa Monica, California. Complication: difficulty swallowing x 3 months.

2. 2007-2010: Multiple PICC line placements. Right upper extremity, left upper extremity. Complications: infections, clotting, bending of the line. Home health nurse.

3. November 2010: Heart catheterization. North Mountain Hospital, Dave Dodds, MD, Cardiology (3130 555-7890. Results: LAD stenosis. No complications.

4. August 2010: Stress thallium test. North Mountain Hospital, Dave Dodds, MD, Cardiology, (3130 555-7890. Results: no stenosis. Normal.

5. August 2001: Caesarian Section: Los Virgenes Hospital, Aurora Fleece, MD, Ob/Gyn, (313) 555-2345. Complications: none.

Appendix D –
Sample of Doctor's SOAP Note

I hope that this encourages you to know your own health better and to help people to understand some medical terminology we doctors have incorporated into our everyday way of life. I expound on this in my book, **The Rebel Patient**, which teaches you how to fight for your diagnosis.

If you understand how doctors think, you will better understand what to do to get the care you deserve.

Below is an example of a "SOAP NOTE" that your doctor enters into the medical record at each visit. Each letter stands for a particular section.

Content in a Doctor's SOAP Note

S – *Subjective*. This is feelings, experience, history.

O – *Objective*. This is math. Vital signs, physical exam, lab results, x-ray or MRI findings, and more.

A – *Assessment*. This is where the doctor analyzes the above and determines a diagnosis. Insurance cannot be billed without it. Each diagnosis is backed up by the subjective and objective findings. All unresolved or continuing diagnoses "stay" with the patient from visit to visit.

P – *Plan*. This takes each Assessment and determines a plan for it. The plan may be lab blood tests, x-rays, supportive measures, prescriptions, referrals to another doctor, and more.

Sample of a Doctor's SOAP Note

S: Forty-three-year-old Hispanic female who looks pale and weak. Complains of nausea and vomiting and is weak and dizzy upon standing.

O:
Vital Signs: Height = 5'4", Weight = 115 lb, Blood Pressure (BP) = 98/67 mm Hg, Heart Rate (HR) = 67 beats/minute (bpm), Respiratory Rate = 14/min, O2 Sat = 98%.

Orthostatics:
Supine: BP = 128/76 mmHg, HR = 81 bpm
Standing: BP = 89/59 mmHg, HR = 133 bpm

Exam:
General: Skin pale, obviously fatigued.
HEENT (Head, Eyes, Ears, Nose, and Throat): Unremarkable.

Lungs: CTA (Clear to Auscultation).

Abdomen: Decreased BS (bowel sounds), no distension. Soft in all four quadrants.

Murphy's Sign negative

Extremities/Integument (Skin): Facial veins prominent, moves all extremities X4.

Rectal: N/A

Neuro: All cranial nerves intact. No limb weakness or sensory loss. Moves all extremities X 4. Reflexes normal.

Labs: UA (Urinalysis): 7.40/leukocyte +/ blood -/ nitrite = +
X-rays: 2019—normal chest x-ray.

A:
1. Dysautonomia
2. Urinary Tract Infection

P:
1. *Dysautonomia*: Continue fluids and high salt intake. Add compression stockings and abdominal binder. Trial of midodrine 5 mg every 4 hours for 3 days. Patient to report back with orthostatics. Do wall exercises shown in clinic.
2. *UTI*: Increase fluid intake. Bactrim DS has worked in the past. Rx Bactrim DS 800/160 mg q12hr x 14 days.

Follow-up: 3 days. Pt to send orthostatics by FAX and she confirmed our FAX number. Then provide another urine sample in 15 days to confirm urine is clear.

For more material on being an advocate while at your doctor's office or in the hospital, stay tuned for Dr. Margaret Aranda's newest book revision, coming soon: *The Rebel `Patient: Fight For Your Care!*

Appendix E –
Bed Exercises

This Appendix is meant to be remembered and/or make a copy and post it next to your bed. Check with your doctor before using.

No one showed me any bed exercises until I had twenty-one hospital admissions. I do not want your body to wither away just because you are bedridden. Keep the muscle that you have and keep the flexibility that you have. Maintaining both attributes can only benefit you in the long run. Do not lay in the hospital bed or your home bed for days or weeks or months without moving around a little bit. A little bit goes a long way, and this is your health, your vitality, and your nonhospital future! You can improve your body strength.

1. Wiggle toes. Widen span of toes and bend the toes up and down. Start out wiggling toes for one minute. May later increase frequency to five to six minutes throughout different parts of the day.

2. Flex and extend ankles. Toes up to the sky, heels on the bed. Then ballet toes to touch the top of the bed, heels off the bed. Keep your buttocks on the bed. Start out doing both ankles together for one minute. May later increase frequency to five to six minutes throughout different parts of the day.

3. Tone calf muscles. As with number 2 above, keep buttocks on the bed. Lift heels up and down a little rapidly. The rest of your foot and toes stay on the bed.

4. Stretch leg muscles. Bring right foot up to your right side, pushing knee down toward the bed. Stretches the quadriceps, your thigh muscles. Repeat on the left leg. Hold the stretch gently, making this a slow-motion movement.

5. Bridging. While on your back, lift your buttocks and thighs off the bed, keeping your feet and lower back on the bed. Make a bridge out of your body pelvis. Tighten when going up, relax and go down. Strengthens your body core (torso) and builds tone in hips and buttocks. Because you are working on your torso, you are improving your sense of balance.

6. Arm and shoulder stretches. Like the swimmer's stretches, gently pull your right elbow across your left chest. Hold for fifteen seconds. Repeat on left arm. Alternate left and right sides, gently holding the stretch.

7. Shoulder and neck stretches. Same as number 6 above, except you are stretching one arm with your elbow above and behind your head. Gently assist with the alternate hand to slightly improve the stretch. Hold stretches for ten seconds and repeat throughout the day to maintain your shoulder's range of motion.

8. Scissoring legs. While on your back, swing legs outward then inward, crisscrossing one leg over the other. Keep toes pointed in ballet position. Helps your inner thighs and hips and gets your blood pumping. Start out with two to three sets and aim for twenty-five counts per set. AKA scissors.

9. Biceps. Sit up and stretch your arms straight out as if you were going to touch the far end of the room. Hands clenched, bring right fist toward your body, perhaps five times. Build up to one hundred, if you can. Repeat with the left arm. AKA biceps builder.

10. Triceps. Don't you just hate it when your upper arms flab in the wind when waving to someone? Stand with your arms straight up, elbows by the ears and palms up. Then lower hands backwards, without moving elbows. Repeat 5-50 times, graduating by holding a can of soup.

Another exercise for triceps: While brushing teeth, do push-ups on the counter. CAUTION: Watch for wet floors, rugs, slippery shoes. Step back a foot, then put palms on edge of counter. Slowly and carefully, lean down putting chin to counter, doing a push-up. Repeat 5-50 times.

Remember: No Falls!

Appendix F – List of Activities of Daily Living (ADLs)

This is a list of activities that describe everyday activities needed for living. If you are deficient in a group of them, you may need a caregiver. If you have long-term disability insurance, your insurance may pay for a caregiver that meets your needs for daily living.

1. Personal Care
   - Bed Bath
   - Shampoo
   - Oral Hygiene
   - Skin Care Lotion
   - Shower
   - Assistance with Dressing
   - Tub Bath
   - Hair Combed

2. Nutrition
   - Meal Preparation
   - Assistance with Feeding

3. Elimination
   - Bedpan
   - Commode
   - Assist to Bathroom
   - Catheter Care
   - Brief Changes

4. Activities
- Standby Assistance
- Transfer Assistance
- Bed Bound Today
- For Bedbound, turn and reposition
- Assist with exercise
- Assist with range of motion /stretching

5. Household
- Shopping/errands
- Laundry
- Light housekeeping
- Change of bed linens

6. Vital Signs

7. Medication Reminders

8. Client Demeanor
- Alert
- Forgetful
- Confused
- Agitated
- Unresponsive

Appendix G –
Sample Incident Report

This is to track dates of incidents including falls, bruising, loss of bowel/bladder function, memory losses, etc. It is not meant to be an all-inclusive list. Please check with your doctor so that you may focus on your personal items.

1. Fall to the
   * Wood flooring
   * Carpet cement
   * Getting into or out of the car

Description of how it happened:

_____
_____
_____
_____
_____

2. Bruise Check (document once a week):
   * Head and neck
   * Arms
   * Torso
   * Buttocks or private parts
   * Legs and toes (measure by cm, where 1 inch = 2.54 cm)

Number of bruises upper body = _____
Number of bruises lower body = _____
Total = _____

3. Other Comments or Observations
   • Contact the patient's family
   • Who spoken to:_____
   • Message left by _____
   • Needs call-back
   • Message left by _____

4. Witnessed by _____ (Signature)
   Print:_____
   Date:_____

5. Call made to doctor_____ Phone_____
6. Call made to nurse_____
   Phone _____
7. Call made to 911_____Time _____
8. Other:

   _____
   _____
   _____
   _____
   _____
   _____

Appendix H –
Patient's Bill of Rights

Can you believe that a Patient's Bill of Rights was first written as an Adoption to the American Hospital Association (AHA) in 1992.

If you ever need to use a hospital, it is comforting for you to know a couple of expectations versus a couple of hospital rules of kindness that are required to be plastered in the open for all to see.

Most certainly, your hospital would have a form that is appropriate for your state. The advance directive may differ and/or add local customs. You could stop in and pick one up in the admissions area or ask the desk information/security officer.

These are excerpts from the American Hospital Association, One North Franklin Street in Chicago, Illinois, 60606. All rights are reserved, and the Catalog number is 157759.

Introduction

Effective health care requires collaboration between patients and physicians and other health care professionals. Open and honest communication, respect for personal and professional values, and sensitivity to differences are integral to optimal patient care. As the setting for the provision of health services, hospitals must provide a foundation for understanding and respecting the rights and responsibilities of patients, their families, physicians, and other caregivers. Hospitals must ensure a health care ethic that respects the role of patients in decision making about treatment choices and other aspects of their care. Hospitals must be sensitive to cultural, racial, linguistic, religious, age, gender, and other differences as well as the needs of persons with disabilities.

The AHA presents a Patient's Bill of Rights with the expectation that it will contribute to more effective patient care and be supported by the hospital on behalf of the institution, its medical staff, employees, and patients. The AHA encourages health care institutions to tailor this Bill of Rights to their patient community by translating and/or simplifying the language of this Bill of Rights as may be necessary to ensure that patients and their families understand their rights and responsibilities.

Bill of Rights. These rights can be exercised on the patient's behalf by a designated surrogate or proxy decision maker if the patient lacks decision-making capacity, is legally incompetent, or is a minor.

1. The patient has the right to considerate and respectful care.

2. The patient has the right to and is encouraged to obtain from physicians and other direct caregivers relevant, current, and understandable information concerning diagnosis, treatment, and prognosis. Except in emergencies when the patient lacks decision making capacity and the need for treatment is urgent, the patient is entitled to the opportunity to discuss and request information related to the specific procedures and/ or treatments, the risks involved, the possible length of recuperation, and the medically reasonable alternatives and their accompanying risks and benefits. Patients have the right to know the identity of physicians, nurses, and others involved in their care, as well as when those involved are students, residents, or other trainees. The patient also has the right to know the immediate and long-term financial implications of treatment choices, insofar as they are known.

3. The patient has the right to make decisions about the plan of care prior to and during the course of treatment and to refuse a recommended treatment or plan of care to the extent permitted by law and hospital policy and to be informed of the medical consequences of this action. In case of such a refusal, the patient is entitled to other appropriate care and series that the hospital provides or transfer to another hospital. The hospital should notify patients of any policy that might affect patient choice within the institution.

4. The patient has the right to have an advance directive (such as a living will, health care proxy, or durable power of attorney for health care) concerning treatment or designating a surrogate decision maker with the expectation that the hospital will honor the intent of that directive to the extent permitted by law and hospital policy. Health care institutions must advise patients of their rights under state law and hospital policy to make informed medical choices, ask if the patient has an advance directive, and include that information in patient records. The patient has the right to timely information about hospital policy that may limit its ability to implement fully a legally valid advance directive.

5. The patient has the right to every consideration of privacy. Case discussion, consultation, examination, and treatment should be conducted so as to protect each patient's privacy.

6. The patient has the right to expect that all communications and records pertaining to his/her care will be treated as confidential by the hospital, except in cases such as suspected abuse and public health hazards when reporting is permitted or required by law. The patient has the right to expect that the hospital will emphasize the confidentiality of this information when it releases it to any other parties entitled to review information in these records.

7. The patient has the right to review the records pertaining to his/her medical care and to have the information explained or interpreted as necessary, except when restricted by law.

8. The patient has the right to expect that, within its capacity and policies, a hospital will make reasonable response to the request of a patient for appropriate and medically indicated care and services. The hospital must provide evaluation, service, and/or referral as indicated by the urgency of the case. When medically appropriate and legally permissible, or when a patient has so requested, a patient may be transferred to another facility. The institution to which the patient must first have accepted the patient for transfer. The patient must also have the benefit of complete information and explanation concerning the need for, risks, benefits, and alternatives to such a transfer.

9. The patient has the right to ask and be informed of the existence of business relationships among the hospital, educational institutions, other health care providers, or payers that may influence the patient's treatment and care.

10. The patient has the right to consent to or decline to participate in proposed research studies or human experimentation affecting care and treatment or requiring direct patient involvement, and to have those studies fully explained prior to consent. A patient who declines to participate in research or experimentation is entitled to the most effective care that the hospital can otherwise provide.

11. The patient has the right to expect reasonable continuity of care when appropriate and to be informed by physicians and other caregivers of available and realistic patient care options when hospital care is no longer appropriate. The patient has the right to be informed of hospital policies and practices that relate to patient care, treatment, and responsibilities. The patient has the right to be

informed of available resources for resolving disputes, grievances, and conflicts, such as ethics committees, patient representatives, or other mechanisms available in the institution. The patient has the right to be informed of the hospital's charges for services and available payment methods.

The collaborative nature of health care requires that patients, or their families/surrogates, participate in their care. The effectiveness of care and patient satisfaction with the course of treatment depend, in part, on the patient fulfilling certain responsibilities. Patients are responsible for providing information about past illnesses, hospitalizations, medications, and other matters related to health status.

To participate effectively in decision making, patients must be encouraged to take responsibility for requesting additional information of clarification about their health status or treatment when they do not fully understand information and instructions. Patients are also responsible for ensuring that the health care institution has a copy of their written advance directive if they have one. Patients are also responsible for informing their physicians and other caregivers if they anticipate problems in following prescribed treatment.

Patients should also be aware of the hospital's obligation to be reasonably efficient and equitable in providing care to other patients and the community. The hospital's rules and regulations are designed to help the hospital meet this obligation.

Patients and their families are responsible for making reasonable accommodations to the needs of the hospital, other patients, medical staff, and hospital employees. Patients are responsible for providing necessary information for insurance claims and for working with the hospital to make payment arrangements, when necessary.

A person's health depends on much more than health services. Patients are responsible for recognizing the impact of their lifestyle on their personal health.

Appendix I

Medical Directives

No More Tears | Dr. Margaret Aranda

A Medical Directive is a template that lists instructions for hospitalization and avoidance of "hospital protocols".

You could seek an attorney, download legal forms, or call your health or state department.

If hospitalized, beware that the staff may "profile" you for their protocols that kill: those who are alone and disabled can be targets. Never go alone. The following offer a list of patient profiles for targeting, as well as a list of orders to refuse.

If you need help in a hospital, seek an advocate by visiting protocolkills.com or GraithCare.com (use Code draranda) or visit our updated sample Medical Directive pinned to my site here: https:// TheRebelPatient.Substack.com

See the following infographics for hospital care:

Profile and Directives

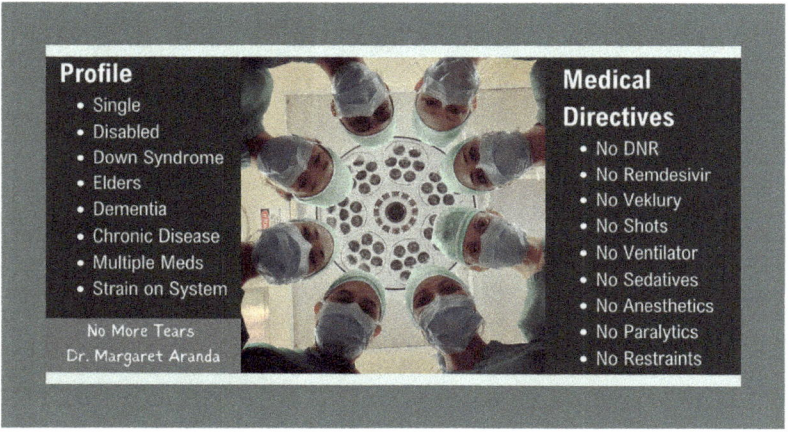

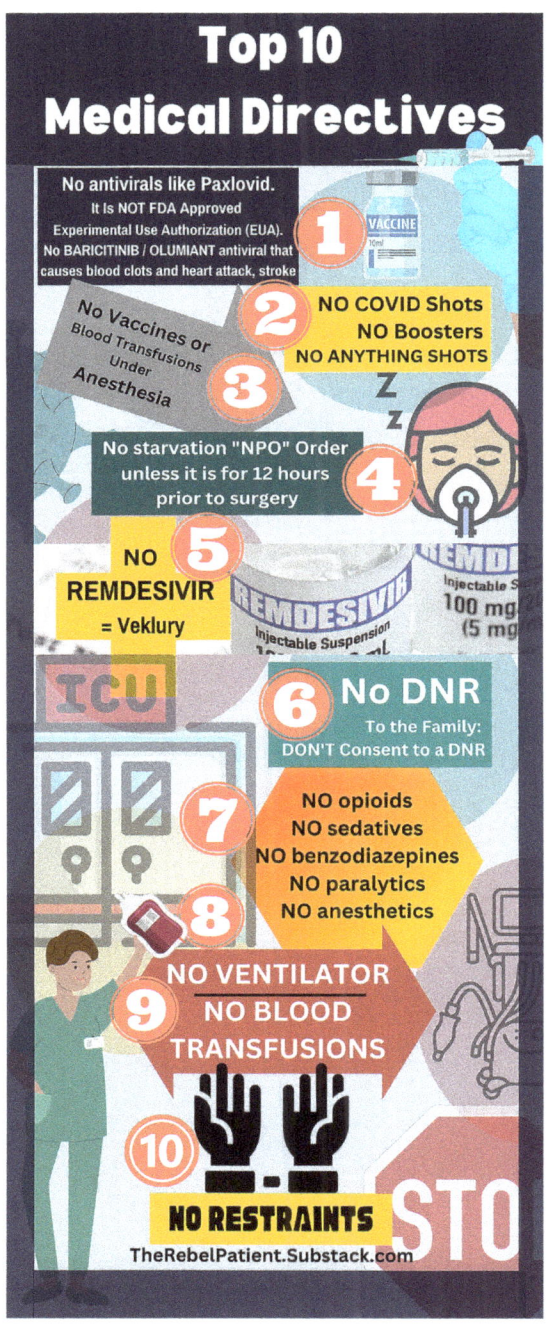

Now it is the moment to have the most serious conversation with you. Forgive me for being blunt, for telling you things you would rather not know.

But remember that I answer to God and my mission is to say what needs to be said. I almost wasn't here. This book was almost not a substance to hold in your hands, or view with your eyes. Please heed my words and I pray they settle on your heart and empower you to have wisdom.

Consider the USA has the highest rates of COVID deaths than any other country in the world. The C.A.R.E.S. Act reimbursed hospitals by diagnosis, allowing lies to perform illegal euthanasia at the tune of 500 to 1000 deaths per day.

Link to Write a Medical Directive in Your State

AARP: https://www.aarp.org/caregiving/financial-legal/ free-printable-advance-directives/Law

Before You Need a Medical Directive

Your best bet is to clarify your wishes in a conversation with your next of kin. Make sure you have an actual conversation and don't just fill out the paperwork without talking to the person who will be making your decisions.

Lastly, some recommend that your orders be notarized with a copy going to your family and your doctor. If this is the case, remember to periodically update it to reflect changes in your decisions.

Perhaps you also would like to have your body ready for donation to a medical school, have your body organs be available for transplantation, and choose your burial or cremation site. This way, your distraught family will not fight over how you want to die, your money, or how you want to be buried.

Please see my Substack for a list of Medical Directives with links to templates in your own state. Because this information also changes with time, refer here for my pinned articles, which are continually updated:

https://therebelpatient.substack.com
https://twitter.com/therebelpatient

Now go.
Live your life one day at a time.
Do not worry about tomorrow.
Just take today and live.

Resources & Links

Resources and Updates from Dr. Margaret Aranda

Blood Transfusions: Blessed By His Blood
https://www.blessedbyhisblood.com/

Email Your Congressional Representatives and Senators:
https://inhere.salsalabs.org/stop-ihr-amendments/index.html

File a Criminal Complaint:
https://www.truthforhealth.org/2022/02/
how-to-file-a-criminal-complaint/

File a Hospital Complaint with the Joint Commission:
https://www.jointcommission.org/resources/patient-safety-topics/
report-a-patient-safety-concern-or-complaint/

File a Medical Board Complaint:
All 50 state medical board complaints:
http://www.neglectreport.com/

Find My Legislator:
https://openstates.org/find_your_legislator/

FREE COVID Care Handout
https://bit.ly/COVIDCareWithTracker

Hospital Hostage Assistance:
https:GraithCare.com and (469) 864-7149 (use CODE "DrAranda")

Hospital Hostage Hotline:
888-C19-EMERGency or 888-219-3637
https://ProtocolKills.com

How Bad Is My Batch (of Vaccine):
https://howbadismybatch.com/

My Substack at The Rebel Patient
https://RebelPatient.Substack.com

My Website:
https://ArandaMDenterprises.com

Petition to Your Congress and get a Medical Freedom Act in the works:
https://alignact.com/go/medical-freedom-act

Report a Sentinel Event:
https://www.truthforhealth.org/report-sentinel-event/

Safe Blood Donation
USA: https://safeblood.us
INTERNATIONAL: safeblood.net
SEARCH FOR A DONOR:
https://safeblood.ch/en/search/

SEARCH FOR A MEDICAL PARTNER:
https://safeblood.net/en/medicialpartner-search/
Twitter: https://Twitter.com/TheRebelPatient

To Be Interviewed by Dr. Aranda on her Rumble, especially for Hospital Death by Remdesivir:
https://rumble.com/c/c-1793991 and/or
email us at:
TheRebelPatient.Substack.com

Links

AFFILIATE LINKS:
(Dr. Aranda's nonprofit receives a small commission):

Augmented NAC
https://augmentednac.com/en | COUPON CODE: HAHV8G4P

Buy Me a Coffee:
https://buymeacoffee.com/dra9

Corganics™: Pharmacy-grade CBD
https://corganics.com
Use CODE "Aranda" (case sensitive)

ECHO H2® WATER
https://lddy.no/1ehe3

How To Win In Court Without a Lawyer:
www.HowToWinInCourt.comrefercode=A
M0060

LifeWave™
Wearable Patch Technology
https://lifewave.com/margaretaranda/store/products

Metagenics Physician-/grade Supplements
https://margaretaranda.metagenics.com
IMMUNE DEFENSE PACK + BENESOM
(MELATONIN)

My Patriot Supply™: https://bit.ly/3a82rik

Renew and Refresh Blog
https://RefreshAndRenew.Substack.com

Speak Life into Your Life Podcast
https://DrMargaretAranda.Substack.com

The Root Labels:
https://therootlabels.com/dra

Write your own substack:
https://substack.com/refer/drmargaretaranda

FREE LINKS:
Alavida®, Pineal Gland Symptoms:
https://www.youtube.com/watch?v=QA7bPPhEeok

Atrial FibrillationAF-Related (Atrial Fibrillation) Stroke Risk Calculator
http://www.preventaf-strokecrisis.org/calculator

Body Mass Index Calculator
https://www.calculator.net/bmi-calculator.html

COVID Care with Tracker®
https://bit.ly/COVIDCareWithTracker

Rumble:
https://rumble.com/v2fs5iy-dr.-james-thorp-landmark-paper-on-covid-19-vaccines-pregnancy-outcomes.html

Substack:
1. *Renew and Refresh:*
   https://renewandrefresh.substack.com

2. *SPEAK LIFE to Your Life:*
   https://drmargaretaranda.substack.com

3. *The Rebel Patient:*
   https:therebelpatient.substack.com

Twitter
1. The Rebel Patient:
   https://twitter.com/therebelpatient

2. Twitter, No More Tears MD:
   https:twitter.com/nomoretearsMD

   Currently banned due to posting VAERS data
   – currently being contested.

Website:
Aranda MD Enterprises
https://arandamdenterprises.com

Dr. Margaret Aranda's Books

**SEE CURRENT AMAZON AND *IN PRESS* BOOKS
WITH MAINSPRING BOOKS**

Guidebook to Spike Protein Detox
In Press with MainSpring Books. COMING SOON!

**Guidebook to Ehlers-Danlos Syndrome:Diagnosis,
Co-Morbidities, and Treatment**
In Press with MainSpring Books. Soon on Amazon!

Guidebook to Growing: For My Daughter
In Press with MainSpring Books. Soon on Amazon!

Guidebook to Low Back Pain: Diagnosis and Treatment
Available in eBook and Paperback on Amazon:
https://amzn.to/3LxEgWW

Little Missy Two-Shoes Likes a Ladybug, Revised Edition
Available in eBook and Paperback on Amazon:
https://amzn.to/3ZPrDxx

Little Missy Two-Shoes Likes To Go To School, Revised Edition
Available in eBook and Paperback on Amazon:
https://amzn.to/3Uj2Twx

The Rebel Patient™: Fight for Your Life!
In Press with MainSpring Books. COMING SOON on Amazon!

EPILOGUE

Dr. Margaret Aranda lives quietly in Southern California. Her daughter is doing well and is a nursing student. Dr. Aranda is engaged to Ed, who loves her more than any man has ever loved her. Her children are her heart, and they will always be her most special souls on earth.

Dr. Aranda is okay, and she will always be okay because no one can take away her miracle from God's light. No one can cause her any more suffering than that which she has already survived.

And with Wayne Connell as President of the Invisible Disabilities Association, she serves as Vice Chair and helps increase awareness of those who appear normal but have damaged bodies.

On September 30, 2022, Dr. Aranda arranged a press release at the steps of the Sacramento capitol steps to ask Governor Newsom to veto bill AB 2098, a bill restricting what doctors can and cannot say to their patients. Ten days later, she received her first accusation from the Medical Board of California, with repeated requests to surrender her license. She surrendered her medical license after two investigators put an envelope under the front door mat at her home.

Dr. Aranda continues to speak at a variety of meetings, summits, and patient advocacy groups, as well as libraries and book clubs.

Dr. Margaret Aranda has a minister's license and visits the sick. She continues to write books. Through it all, her biggest desire is for God to continue to open the doors that need to be opened and to close the doors that need to be closed. And her greatest possessions are stored: as treasures in heaven. She is richer beyond all measure by bearing two children, a boy and a girl. At the final edits of this book, Dr. Aranda typed with one arm, after the non-dominant arm was broken by a large dog at a park.

When she tells people how she persevered through the tremulous times of her life, this is what she says: "God is always with me."

"At my first defense, no one stood at my side, but everyone deserted me. May it not be counted against them. But the Lord stood at my side so that through me the message might be fully proclaimed, and unbelievers might hear of my story.

And I was rescued from the lion's mouth!

The Lord will rescue me from every evil attack and will bring me safely into his heavenly kingdom!

To God be the glory, forever and ever!

Amen!"

2 Timothy 4:16

www.ingramcontent.com/pod-product-compliance
Lightning Source LLC
Chambersburg PA
CBHW051258120626
46547CB00015B/1996